Tennis: The Bassett System

Glenn Bassett

with Terry Galanoy

HENRY REGNERY COMPANY • CHICAGO

Library of Congress Cataloging in Publication Data

Bassett, Glenn.
    Tennis: the Bassett system.

    Includes index.
    1. Tennis.   I. Galanoy, Terry, joint author.
II. Title.
GV995.B38   1977   796.34′22   76-55670
ISBN 0-8092-7916-9

All photos by Norm Schindler

Copyright © 1977 by Glenn Bassett
All rights reserved
Published by Henry Regnery Company
180 North Michigan Avenue, Chicago, Illinois 60601
Manufactured in the United States of America
Library of Congress Catalog Card Number: 76-55670
International Standard Book Number: 0-8092-7916-9

Published simultaneously in Canada by
Beaverbooks
953 Dillingham Road
Pickering, Ontario L1W 1Z7
Canada

Contents

Introduction: If You Can Count to Four, You Can Win at Tennis

1. Ground Strokes   1
   Forehand 1
   Backhand 8
   Passing Shots 15
   Lobs 20
   Approach Shot 27
   Drop Shot 31
   Two-Handed Stroke 34

2. Serves   41
   Grip 42
   Stance 42
   Ready Position 42
   Bassett System for the Serve 43
   Practice 46
   Strategy 46
   Return of Serve 47

3. Net Play   57
   Volley 57
   Half Volley 64
   Overhead Smash 67
   Backhand Overhead 70

4. Position and Footwork   73
   Position 73
   Footwork 77

5. Equipment   83
   Rackets 83
   Tennis Balls 85
   Shoes 86
   Clothing 86
   Other Equipment 87

6. Secrets of Practice   89
   Practicing for Tournaments 91

7. Questions and Answers about Winning Strategy   93
   How to Win Even If You Lose 97

Glossary   99

Index   103

ABOUT GLENN BASSETT

You have to be one of the best in the world to be head coach of the championship UCLA tennis team—and Glenn Bassett is. In 1950, when Bassett was ranked fifth in national collegiate listings, he cocaptained the UCLA team to its first National Collegiate Athletic Association (NCAA) championship. Later, he coached at California's Santa Monica High School, turning in a record performance of 142 wins against only 2 losses in a six-year period. So formidable were his high school teams that Santa Monica became known as the "tennis champion factory," producing scores of top-ranked amateurs, many of whom later became professionals. Bassett returned to UCLA in 1965 as assistant coach and two years later was appointed head coach of that traditionally awesome Bruin squad.

During his years in this position, Bassett's teams have captured four NCAA championships, and won the tough Pacific Eight Conference Championship six out of ten times, playing against such nationally ranked powerhouses as Stanford University and the University of Southern California.

Included in the crowds of top tennis players trained by Bassett (either as assistant or head coach) are Jimmy Connors, Arthur Ashe, Billy Martin, Charlie Pasarell, Ian Crookenden, Roy Barth, Jeff Borowiak, Haroon Rahim, Jeff Austin, Bob Kreiss, Steve Krulevitz, Brian Teacher, Peter Fleming, and other consistent winners in world, national, and local play.

Perhaps the highest compliment to his coaching effectiveness and to "The Bassett System" was his selection as Intercollegiate Tennis Coach of the Year by the other tennis teachers who make up the Intercollegiate Tennis Coaches Association. Bassett has also been awarded dozens of cups, scrolls, trophies, and ribbons by tennis publications, sporting goods manufacturers, private and public tennis groups, and athletic associations for the continuing fine performance of his teams and for his unique and effective coaching methods.

Those methods—which make up the simple but highly effective *Bassett System*—have, until now, been restricted exclusively to members of Bassett's tennis squads. This is the first time Bassett has consented to share his total package of winning secrets with the tennis-playing public at large.

In the following pages the Bassett System is clearly, easily, and completely explained so that you can also learn to play tennis like Jimmy Connors or, at least, like a member of Bassett's intercollegiate championship UCLA squads.

Introduction: If You Can Count to Four, You Can Win at Tennis

When you see a coach huddled with a top-ranked amateur or professional player during tournament play, he is not usually giving out sly, super-secret tips of slick strategy. What he is generally doing is reminding that experienced player to *bend his knees more, watch the ball longer,* or to *complete his follow through.* All basics. And all basically the simple secrets of winning at tennis. The types of rackets, types of balls, court surfaces, strategies, and even philosophies of play all come in a poor second in importance to mastering the one idea of the game: proper fundamentals. Once you've learned them, you've learned a good 85 percent of what tennis is all about.

That's also what 85 percent of this book is about. The other 15 percent gets into some ideas and concepts of advanced tennis techniques and strategies used by coaches and players who consistently win. I've even included the physical fitness programs, psychologies, and playing-to-win tips I've learned and have been using during my twenty-five years of involvement with competition tennis. I guess you could call this book an *advanced* basic book or a *basic* advanced book, depending upon whether you're an A, B, C, or D player, a beginner, or even a coach or teaching pro.

Through my early years, as a player and as a coach, I began wondering why some players took naturally to the game while others who seemed to have the same athletic abilities continued to play hit-and-miss tennis regardless of how much instruction they took and how long they practiced. I wondered why some team players were better than others. I even wondered why some ten-year olds became good enough to play high school or college tournament tennis after only a short time of playing the game. And, I wondered why some fifty-five-year olds, who had lost much of their youthful reflexes and speed and stamina, could still whip good younger players. I began searching for some answers. After all, nobody is born a natural tennis player. It's a game and through the years it has developed a pattern of physical attitudes and actions which, when followed properly, give the player the most effective performance. Yes, I know there are variations; two-handed backhands, two-handed forehands; I've even seen ambidextrous players, who literally throw the racket from one hand to the other giving them two forehands and no backhand, and I've seen some of these noncomformists win, consistently.

After years of working with players of all ages and all variations of natural athletic ability, I finally realized that the basic secret of winning tennis was (a) learning the strokes and (b) most importantly, developing a natural rhythm for those strokes. The players who never seemed to improve were those who had the movements down pat but who couldn't seem to get the timing. Yet, it is that very timing which makes the strokes work. There is no accuracy or no power or no control if the body, the arm, and the racket are not coordinated for maximum effect. Further, I realized that much of tennis coordination is not natural to the body and must be learned. Out of this, I began breaking down each important tennis movement into its component parts and giving them a definite pace and count. Within each count, I then broke down the action that should take place. Suddenly, a "system" was born.

The backbone of the material which follows is what my players and some other coaches have kindly come to call The Bassett System. As much as I'd like to take credit for coming up with a totally revolutionary idea in tennis technique, I really can't. This system is actually a simple but proven rhythm-in-reflex process that removes the contradictions and confusions you've learned in the past and replaces them with a smooth harmonious process for control of yourself, the ball, and the game.

With this method every stroke, even the serve, is broken down into an elementary *one-two-three-four* count. *When you learn these and exactly what happens on each count*, you'll be on your way to a better, more satisfying, victorious game.

Because I feel that this method is the most important tennis lesson I can offer, I have placed it first in these pages and have stayed with it in complete and thorough detail for most of the book. The types of rackets, types of balls, conditioning procedures, the psyching-out of opponents, the advanced strategies of percentage tennis have been placed at the rear of this book. In short, the information here is put down in what I consider the order of importance to me as a coach and to you as a player.

Remember, as I've told my teams and players for years, if you can count to four, you can win. The following pages will prove it's just that simple.

Glenn Bassett

I. Ground Strokes

Because most youngsters in this country learn to swing a baseball bat before they learn to swing a tennis racket, the forehand is the easiest stroke for a *beginner* to learn. However, the *advanced* player finds that it becomes harder and harder to master it. If that seems curious, I'll explain why it isn't.

During the early stages of tennis playing, beginners learn to hit to their opponent's backhand, and logically they have a high percentage of returns hit to their backhand. Nearly all of the pros and instructors and coaches point out that the backhand is generally a new player's weakest ground stroke and that "sure putaway points" can be had just by aiming at that side. So what happens? Faced with a continuing barrage of balls hit to the backhand side, that player begins developing a strong backhand. The forehand deteriorates because of lack of concentration on it. Suddenly, what used to be the most effective, strongest ground stroke has become the weakest. Yet, the forehand should be at least as strong as the backhand.

BASSETTIP: *Even if you feel that your forehand doesn't need work, practice it anyway. Like anything else, you either use it or lose it.*

FOREHAND

You have probably been told how to hold your racket at least 100 times. Bear with me while I go into it for the 101st time so we can start out together. Some of you may be familiar with the information that follows. Most of you may find a surprise or two.

If you want to play well and win, one of the first and most important requirements is to feel the ball on your racket. No feel, no control. It's that simple. Holding the racket properly to get that feel is simple too, once you learn how.

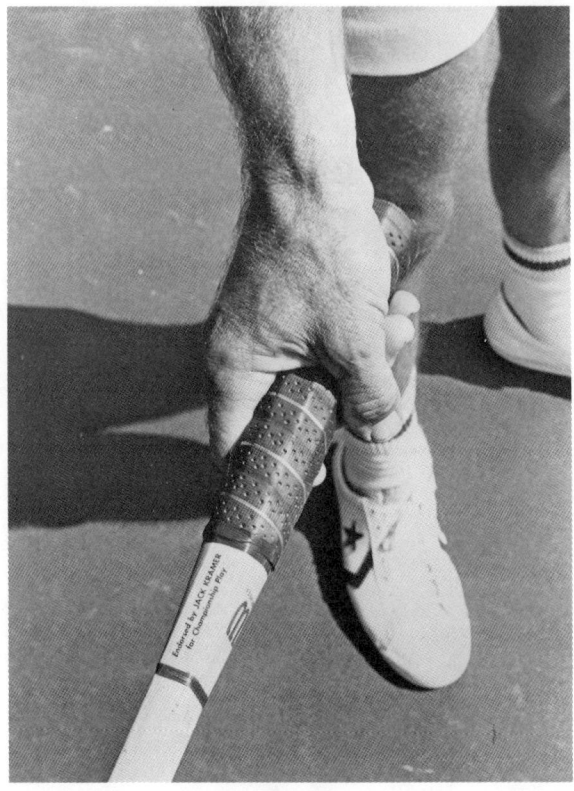
Eastern Grip

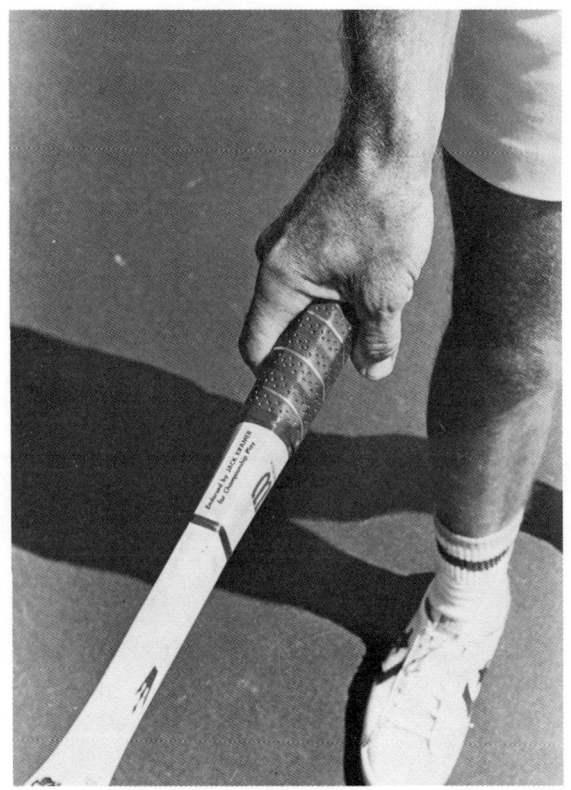
Continental Grip

As others may have told you, you do *not* hold the racket in a handshake position. What they might not have told you is that the racket is *held with the fingers and not with the hand*! First, spread your fingers comfortably, take the racket in that handshake position with the racket held primarily by your index and middle fingers, both relaxed. If you hold these fingers too tightly around the racket handle, you will lose the feel of the ball and the continual tension and strain will soon tire your hand, arm, and shoulder. Also, relaxed fingers help you move the racket faster when you have to shift it for a backhand shot.

BASSETTIP: *The racket is properly held by the index and middle fingers, both relaxed. The remainder of the hand supports and cushions the shot. A dull sound to your shot means the racket is being held too tightly.*

There are basically three types of forehand grips; the *eastern*, the *western*, and the *continental*, which is really a forehand-backhand compromise. Each grip has its advantages and disadvantages. I like the eastern forehand grip for beginners and intermediate players. It provides feel, control, and the right angle to the racket head when it is swung properly.

The eastern grip is physically closer to the continental grip used by many advanced players. As your game improves you might want to switch to it. The advantage of the continental is that no grip change is necessary for forehand or backhand shots and this can be crucial in a fast game. However, strokes from a continental grip do tend to be weaker because it is harder to hit the ball at the proper place; out in front of your body.

The western grip moves your hand backwards away from the eastern and continental grips. This one is used mostly

GROUND STROKES

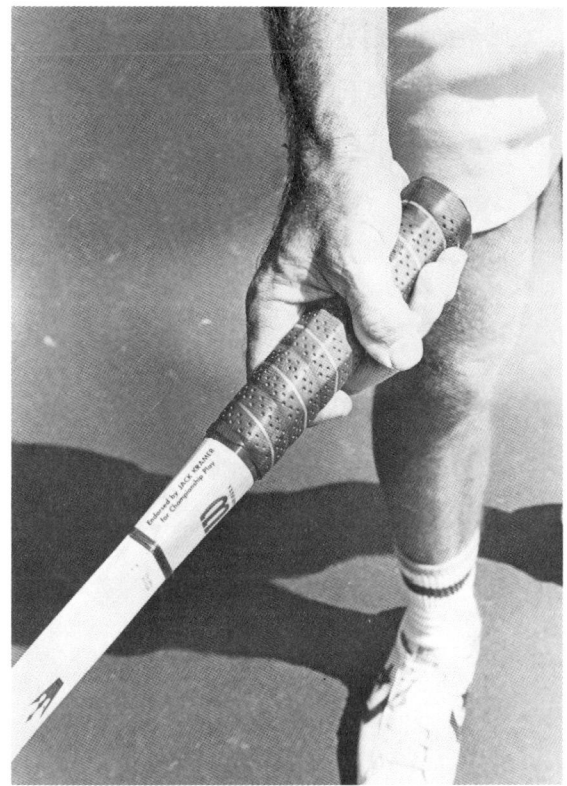

Western Grip

Ready Position

by clay court players who want to hit high, bouncing balls with a lot of top spin on them. I don't recommend the western because you can't get good depth with the amount of top spin it puts on the ball. It is also harder to hit low, bouncing balls with your hand and racket in that position.

THE BASSETT FOREHAND SYSTEM

In the introduction to this book, I mentioned that the system I use and teach is so simple that if you can count to four you can win. It works for every stroke; forehand, backhand, approach shot, volley, serve, every one. The following explains how it works for your forehand. There may seem to be a lot of complicated instructions. There are not. Your body and natural reflexes will do most of them automatically. I have gone into detail, however, so you can easily pick out the times and places that are throwing off your natural forehand stroke. The single most important thing to remember is the one-two-three-four rhythm of the forehand and what happens with each count.

Count One: Backswing

If you wait to start your backswing until the ball gets to you, or even until it crosses the net, you're also going to wait a long time to develop a winning game. Even the best players with the fastest reflexes start their backswings as soon as they see the ball coming off the opponent's racket. The backswing should be finished and in place by the time you get into position to return the ball. For beginners, intermediates, and even those advanced players who are having trouble meeting the ball in front of them, I recommend a short, straight backswing. You can run faster and easier to the ball contact point when your racket isn't making arcs in the air or so far back you're out of control and off balance as you move across the court. After you have mastered the straight-back backswing and are more advanced, you can use a circular figure eight backswing if you like.

The straight-back backswing starts with the racket head moving backwards perpendicular or slightly closed to the ground—with the racket head and not the arm moving first. To do this, bend the wrist back a little from the arm, so the head of the racket actually leads the backswing. This will give power to your return. During this part of the backswing, your arm is also slightly bent at the elbow and fairly close to the body. Take the racket head back a little lower than your wrist if you're going after a normal or low bouncing ball but slightly higher than your wrist for high bouncing balls. If the ball is going to have a great deal of bounce, lift your entire arm slightly.

For you intermediate and advanced players who use the circular or figure eight backswing, the racket head should go back higher than your wrist and your wrist should go back higher than your elbow. The advantages to the circular or figure eight backswing are more rhythm and more power; but you get less control, and it takes more time. Beginners who try it are usually still in the middle of some fancy aerobatic swing as the ball goes breezing by. Startled, they swing suddenly, hit late, and usually send the ball over the fence—not for a home run but for a run to the backyard of someone's home to fetch it.

Many players, even better ones, make the mistake of moving their elbow too much. At the start of the backswing, the elbow is in *front* of the hip and at the finish of the backswing it has moved only to the *back* of the hip and a few inches away from it. At the end of the backswing, your arm is still relaxed and bent slightly at the elbow and wrist. Your right or hitting shoulder is turned slightly back and open.

Forehand Backswing

(For lefthanded players, please transpose and translate.)

The left hand, for right-handed players, has an important job in the backswing. Too many players let it flop around instead of using it as an important part of the backswing. Ideally, the left hand stays on the racket, in a cradling position, for six to twelve inches at the start of the backswing. This helps guide the racket back and also forces the left shoulder around just enough so you can develop the most power and control. Too much body turn for beginners and intermediates can affect that control and power by forcing you into a cramped position. Advanced players, of course, begin to turn sideways more and more as the timing improves.

When the left hand slides away from the racket, it should move out naturally and easily toward the oncoming ball. This helps balance your body and gives you the hand-eye communication with

Forehand Step

the ball, which helps keep it in front of you.

Your body should look like a comma during the backswing. Your knees should be slightly bent (for normal shots and a great deal for low ones). Your body should be bent slightly forward from the waist. And your head should be bent forward so your eyes are as much on a level with the ball as possible. Try not to bend over with your back, but use your knees to get down. This helps you see the ball and get under it. Form a close triangle with your head, left hand, and right hand forming the angles of the triangle. This is important!

BASSETTIP: *Try not to strangle the racket handle in a hammerlock. Hold it tightly enough for control but loose enough to get the feel of the ball.*

Count Two: Step

The front foot: Just before you want to make contact with the oncoming ball, step forward with your front foot making sure you don't overstride or throw yourself off balance. Your head and body will move forward naturally, and the weight of your body will shift from the back leg to the front one. Push off the back leg to get onto the front leg. Make sure the body doesn't lean out over the front leg. When possible, make sure the front foot steps in the direction you want your ball to go.

This step forward gives you more of an "opened up" position. The racket now moves farther back (to where it started) so that it is 180 degrees or perpendicular to the net. Letting the racket head get farther around than that can give you more power but can affect control. Advanced players can master it, but beginners and intermediates should work more on that control. Although your elbow is still slightly bent and relaxed, the step forward will automatically straighten the arm a little and move the elbow farther away from the right hip. Your wrist is still laid back a little from your arm and the racket head is lower than the spot where you plan to hit the ball and perpendicular or closed slightly to the ground. If you're planning a top spin return, the racket head should be slightly turned toward the ground or "closed."

The other arm remains in front of you still pointing at the ball and still relaxed.

Move your head forward with the body, but do not lift it. It remains eye level to the ball.

BASSETTIP: *Shift weight from the back leg to the front leg, making sure your body doesn't shift too far forward and throw you into an off balance reaching position.*

Count Three: Hit

There are two main places for your racket head to meet the ball. If you want to return the ball *crosscourt* to the opponent, your racket should connect with the ball when it is six to twelve inches in front

Forehand Hit

of your front foot. If you want the ball to go straight or *down the line*, hit it six or less inches in front of that front foot. Always connect before the ball has passed the front foot. When rallying or practicing try to hit a high percentage of forehands crosscourt because this helps you learn how to hit the ball in front of you.

The racket arm: When the racket head starts forward to meet the ball it moves out and away from your body, also carrying your elbow out and away. (This is called an "inside-out" hit because your racket starts close and then moves out from your hip.) The arm is still slightly bent at the start of the forward movement, but it straightens as it approaches the ball. By the time you hit the ball the racket arm is nearly, but not totally, straight. The racket head should be moving upwards on a diagonal so it will lift the ball up and over the net. On high or bouncing balls use less lift, but make sure you use some. (Many players beat themselves simply by putting the ball into the net and losing points.) In addition to the upward movement of the racket head, it should contact the ball in one of three angles; closed, open, or perpendicular. If you want to return the ball with a lot of top spin or hit a high bouncing return, hit it with the racket face "closed" or turned toward the ground. If you are hitting low balls or want to slice your return, angle the racket head more toward the sky (open). On normal bouncing balls that you want to return flat and with power, keep the racket head straight (perpendicular) up and down. In team and individual instruction, I try to discourage slice forehand groundstrokes.

At the moment of contact, the racket head should catch up with the wrist and arm. Wrist, arm, and racket should be *parallel to the net if you want your shot to go down the line* or *a little diagonal to the net if you want to place your shot crosscourt*.

The racket hand fingers tighten naturally at the moment of contact. They should grip the racket securely enough so it does not twist or turn in your hand but not so tightly that you lose the feel of the ball.

The body and head do not straighten up as the racket moves diagonally up and through the ball. Keep that comma position, and make sure your head is down and your eyes stay as level with the ball as they can. The head will move forward naturally but should not move up.

The shoulders and hips also move forward with the stroke, but the rear leg stays back; the heel lifting from the ground and the toe dragging. Try to keep that rear foot touching the ground. If it lifts completely, it can throw you off balance and affect your return.

BASSETTIP: *Keep your eyes on the ball all the way into the strings of your racket and back out again.*

Count Four: Follow Through

Follow through on your forehand

Forehand Follow Through

stroke gives you accurate placement and power. Regardless of how many times I say this, many players continue to poke and punch at the ball or pull up short just after making contact. Their forehands hit the net, go out of the court, or plop down like sitting ducks to be blasted away. The fourth count or follow through is the payoff, the most important part of the entire one-two-three-four count.

The most important part of the follow through is keeping your racket on the ball —in a straight line—for six inches to a foot after you meet it. This gives the ball direction and power.

The racket arm goes through the ball absolutely straight now. The right shoulder comes forward until it is ahead of your left shoulder. The left shoulder has not moved and is not pulled back during the follow through. At the finish your head is still down; your right shoulder swings through until it touches your chin and remains there through the finish. The racket finishes higher than your head.

The left arm stays in front and never pulls away from the body. It ends up underneath the right arm at the finish.

The legs begin straightening after you have stayed with the ball six inches to a foot. They should be completely straight at the finish with all of your weight on the front foot. This gives you additional power and a natural top spin. Your head also moves up with the body but continues looking at the ball with rapt attention. If you lift your head too soon, the movement of the racket will be affected, and you will lose communication with the ball.

The wrist can be rolled over slightly, but do not flick or break it because it will affect your accuracy.

The only time you tighten your fingers on the racket grip is during the hit and follow through. You tighten them only enough to keep the racket from slipping out of your hand or twisting. Remember to keep your fingers relaxed enough to get the feel of the ball all the time it is on the racket.

After you complete the forehand follow through, you should *freeze* for a second or two to check yourself. Do this every time you practice, and it will soon become a natural habit you will use in play.

Check the following points:

1. Is your weight on the left leg?
2. Is your right leg back, dragging forward a little?
3. Is your left arm forward, close to your body and under your right arm?
4. Is your right shoulder forward, ahead, higher than the left?
5. Are your eyes looking at the ball?
6. Is your racket arm straight?
7. Is your racket higher than your head (the amount higher depends upon top spin)?
8. Has the racket head been thrown out in the direction of the hit?
9. Has the momentum carried the

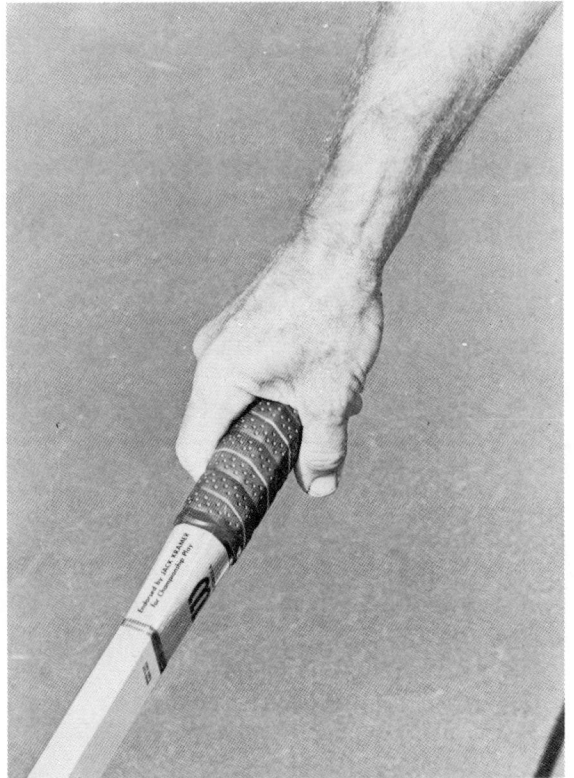

Continental Grip

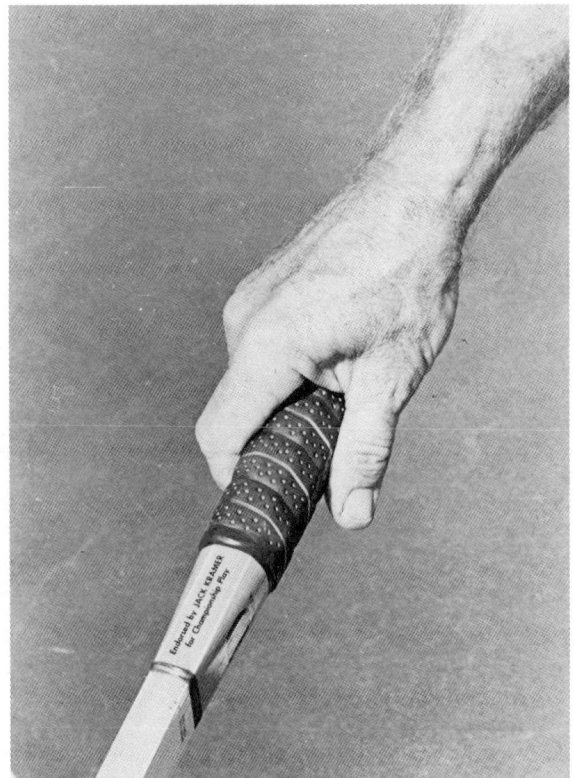

Eastern Backhand Grip

racket head slightly across of the intended line of hit?
10. Has the top edge of the racket been slightly rolled over ahead of the bottom edge?

BACKHAND

The backhand (if I may mix my bodily references) is the Achilles' heel of many beginners. But there's no reason for this to be so. For the beginner the backhand movement provides a much more natural away-from-the-body swing for control and power when meeting the ball. For intermediate and advanced players, the backhand should be as easy, natural, and effective as the forehand because (a) most serious players practice it a great deal and (b) because most opponents hit to it often. Tennis, like all racket sports, is one-handed game played from two sides of the body. Without a good backhand the player is not only handicapped for 50 percent of the time but is going to be handicapped all of the time as soon as the opponent learns of that weakness. Regardless of how strong your forehand is, you cannot hope to "run around" all shots to return them with your forehand. First of all, it takes too much time to move around to the forehand side, and secondly, an opponent who is accurate can drive you right off the court with a series of shots you should be handling with your backhand. There is only one solution: Learn the backhand and continue to practice it—against backboards, against friends, against opponents—until it's as good as your forehand. Many players find that after they've learned the backhand properly, it actually becomes their best and strongest stroke.

There are two grips you can use for the backhand stroke. The first is that combination forehand-backhand-serve grip called the continental. Quite a few tournament players like this grip because it doesn't have to be changed for different strokes. In today's fast-paced competition with hard-hit balls and instant volleying, the continental grip does save those important split-seconds. Also, I've always felt that the slice return (we'll get into details on this later in the chapter) is handled a bit easier with the continental.

However, for all around driving power for the flat return and for control of the top spin return, I prefer the eastern backhand grip even though it does take a second or so to change from the forehand to the eastern backhand. The eastern backhand grip also gives you more power, whether you use top spin, flat drive, or slice.

The backhand, like the forehand, falls easily and simply into four basic movements or counts: the backswing, the step, the hit, and the follow through. There are many similarities in these movements between the forehand and the backhand, and there are *many differences* as well. It is those differences that can change a weak, inaccurate backhand into a strong attacking weapon.

Count One: Backswing

Like the forehand, you start your backswing as soon as you see the ball leave your opponent's racket, and like the forehand that backswing should be finished by the time you get into position to return the ball. For that reason, I usually encourage players to develop a short, straight backswing, which permits you to run without pulling you backwards or off balance. Beginners (or players who have difficulty hitting the ball in front of them) should take the racket back straight. Advanced players can use the circular or figure eight backswing for more power and rhythm but should remember that it does take more time and can create a loss of control.

Backhand Backswing

The racket arm does not go back first for the straight-back backswing. The racket head does. The wrist is bent open a little, allowing the racket head to move back ahead of and lower than the wrist. The wrist is lower than the elbow. Both elbow and wrist are slightly bent. (For the circular or figure eight backswing, the racket head goes back *higher* than the wrist and the wrist goes back *higher* than the elbow.)

The left hand has two important jobs during the backswing. If you are going to change from the forehand grip to the eastern backhand, the left hand cradles and supports the racket approximately halfway up the shaft while you turn the racket approximately one-eighth of a turn. Take the racket back slightly open and perpendicular to the ground. Your thumb can also be placed in a diagonal position on the grip at this time (although this is controversial; some pros say it does more harm to your control than good). The second job of the left hand is to lead the racket back until it is about even with your left hip. Fingers of the left hand are cupped and under the racket someplace between the middle and the top of the shaft. The left hand stays in that position until you begin Count Three of the swing to hit the ball. Your left and right hands and your head again form a close triangle at the conclusion of Count One and your body forms a comma position.

Turn your body a little sideways to the net and stay in the comma position with the weight on the left or back leg; knees bent and relaxed. Your eyes should be on a level with the oncoming ball.

Count Two: Step

Like the forehand the correct point of contact with the ball should be six to twelve inches in front of your front foot if you want to hit the ball crosscourt and six inches or less in front of that foot if you want to hit it straight down the line.

Judging by the speed of the oncoming ball, begin your forward step so that you will contact the ball at the proper distance from the front foot.

The front or right foot (for you right-handers) steps in the direction you want the ball to go; all of your body weight shifts from the back foot onto the front. Be careful not to overstride and throw yourself too far forward and off balance. Also be sure to shift that weight forward to the front leg to gain maximum stroke power. As you step forward, the racket (with both hands still on it) will automatically go back a bit more, completing your backswing and putting you into a tight, coiled-up position. Some players do get the racket back more than 180 degrees to the net to gain more power but there is some loss of control for all but the advanced players.

Backhand Step

The racket arm automatically straightens out more as you step forward. The elbow is still slightly bent and a few inches from your stomach. The wrist is still bent slightly, and at this point it allows the racket head to drop slightly so it will connect under the ball during the hit.

The body and head move forward naturally as you step forward, the body stopping when it is balanced over the right forward leg, the head out in front of that leg, as low to eye level with the oncoming ball as you can get. The head does not lift when it comes forward but concentrates on staying in eye contact with the ball. Although the head does move ahead of the front leg, make sure it does not pull the body too far, creating an off balance condition which will have you reaching for the ball.

BASSETTIP: *Both hands remain on the racket all the way through Count Two.*

Count Three: Hit

Where you hit the ball and how you hit it is crucial to the backhand. Many players who seem to have the form down perfectly still can't get the ball back accurately or with power. They are hitting too early, too late, or with the racket head in the wrong position and location. Yet, the backhand hit should be natural, easy-flowing movement that gives you mastery of the return.

As I said, the proper point of contact between the racket head and the ball should be six to twelve inches in front of your front foot if want the ball to go crosscourt and six inches or less if you want the ball to go straight or down the line. Remember, if the ball gets past your front foot before you hit, you're late and you've lost control and power . . . and maybe the ball.

Timing yourself from that intended point of contact, just as the racket arm starts forward, the left hand finally leaves the racket shaft. The right arm is slightly bent at first but straightens out as the racket gets closer to the ball. By the time you contact the ball your arm should be almost straight, the racket parallel to the net (but not the arm). Properly done, the arm is diagonal to the net at the moment of contact.

As you move the racket forward, it moves naturally out and away from your body in that inside-out stroke I mentioned in the forehand. The racket is moving upward and forward in a diagonal motion so it will lift the ball up and over the net. For high, bouncing balls you don't need as much upward motion and can keep the racket more parallel to the ground.

As soon as the racket starts to move forward, adjust the head angle for the oncoming ball. For low balls, bend those knees and get down so the racket can get under them. Get the head of the racket

Backhand Hit

below your waist, and turn your wrist slightly so the bottom edge leads, and your racket is in an open position. For medium bouncing balls close the racket slightly by turning it straighter up and down. And for high balls adjust the racket so it comes forward above your waist and with the head closed and the top edge of the racket head leading slightly or at least even with the bottom one.

For crosscourt shots, the racket head must connect with the ball when it is slightly ahead of your wrist. Down the line shots are made when wrist and racket are in a straight line and parallel to the net.

Tighten your fingers at the moment of contact so the racket won't twist or turn in your hand, but make sure you don't get a hammer lock on the grip and lose the feel of the ball.

Your body uncoils naturally as the racket arm swings through the hit, but it does not straighten up. Too many players, even competition-trained ones, develop the bad habit of lifting their entire bodies during this part of the stroke. That jerks the racket up instead of *through* the ball, and the ball generally ends up in the net and is an easy putaway for your opponent. Remember to keep your eyes on the ball steadily and continually until it comes into and back out of the racket strings. Although your head moves forward the eyes concentrate on the ball.

As the hit movement uncoils, your right shoulder moves forward in the intended direction of your hit and the hips begin to turn to face the net. Your weight is on the ball of your front foot and the left toe begins to drag a little, the heel lifting naturally from the ground.

BASSETTIP: *Make sure your racket head is moving forward and up. This gives you top spin, which keeps the ball in the court. It also keeps you from driving the ball into the net for an unnecessary loss of points.*

Count Four: Follow Through

I'll give you an inside tip. You can make a lot of mistakes on Counts One, Two, and Three, but if you follow through correctly, your shot has a good chance of making it. The most important part of the follow through is keeping the racket head in contact with the ball. If you hold the ball in the racket for six inches after you make contact, you're well on your way to power and control. If you merely brush across it, the ball will probably go everywhere but where you want it. To do this, it is necessary to develop that *feel* in your fingers. When the racket head meets the ball, *feel* it there, and hold that racket steady and smoothly straight through that six-inch part of the follow through. Aim it exactly where you want the ball to go. At the end of that six-inch movement, the arm and fingers begin moving the racket diagonally up and out. Your intent is to finish with the racket aimed exactly where you want the ball to go, but the natural momentum of the swing will carry it beyond that point. The racket moves across your body and finishes higher than your head, arm straight. Your arm rolls over slightly while it straightens. The top edge of the racket head will turn slightly over and be ahead of the bottom edge. Make sure you don't flick or break your wrist and lose control of the follow through stroke.

As your hitting arm goes forward, your right shoulder moves forward also until the arm is straight. At that point it moves up and around, opening up your body so you are now facing the net at a forty-five-degree angle. The arm and shoulder movement together gives you the power you need for a strong backhand return. Meanwhile, the left shoulder swings forward a little but always stays in back of the right one. At the finish of the stroke, your right shoulder is higher than the left, pulled there by the upraised racket, which is now higher than your head.

When your left arm drops away from the racket at the beginning of the swing, it moves behind your body, palm facing the ground and lower than your left shoulder. This arm helps you keep balance.

As the racket head moves across your body, your knees and legs begin straightening up in a lifting movement that will give you additional power plus a natural top spin that will help keep the return in the court. As your body straightens up, so does the head, but it remains forward of the body. Make sure you don't lift your head too soon and destroy a good shot.

At the very end all your weight is over the front leg, the back leg dragging a little to maintain your balance. As with the forehand, hold your final position a second or two to check it and to make sure you are balanced. Make a habit of check-

GROUND STROKES 13

Backhand Follow Through

ing your final follow-through position. It will become an automatic reflex and a constant reminder to you of the proper form for the backstroke.

Look for these points:

Is your weight on your right leg?
Is your left leg still back? (It comes forward a little.)
Is your left arm behind your body?
Is your right shoulder higher than your left and opened up a little to face the net?
Is your head forward and over your body in a comma position?
Is your right arm straight?
Have your hips turned so they face the net a little?
Is your racket head higher than your head?
Has the racket head moved past the point of the intended shot?
Is the top edge of the racket head slightly ahead of the bottom edge?

BASSETTIP: *Concentrate on keeping the ball on the strings for six inches after making contact with it. This is the single most important part of the follow through stroke and gives you the drive and accuracy you need for an effective return.*

THE BACKHAND SLICE

So far we have been working with the backhand drive; the shot that gives you both power and depth. Depth is probably the most important advantage you can give your ground strokes.

However, the backhand slice should definitely be part of your collection of ground strokes. You will need it a great deal in competition play. For example, when you have to hit a ball on the rise, a slice will put more of your racket strings on that ball and give you more control than a standard drive stroke. That's because the strings are actually coming down on the ball in the slice instead of moving up and across it as in a drive.

I've also learned that it's easier to hit high, bouncing balls with the slice because you can get your racket head higher and still get away a powerful return.

Also, the slice can become your backup stroke for those times (and it happens to every player) when your drive isn't working and you've lost confidence in it. When you do lose your backhand drive stroke (and one of the unsolved mysteries even to tennis coaches is why it does come and go even with the best of players) and are losing points and games and your tennis self-esteem, drop the drive and switch to the slice immediately. Then, as you begin to pick up your confidence—maybe in the same set or match or day—start going back to your drive again. Don't, however, get in the habit of depending upon the slice as your bread and butter backhand. It cannot give nor ever will give you the power and depth of the backhand drive.

14 TENNIS: THE BASSETT SYSTEM

Backhand Slice Backswing

Backhand Slice Step

Even if your backhand drive is working well, there are two times you might want to play the percentages by using your slice. The first occurs when you have an opponent who doesn't like the way the slice return stays low, and skips across the court surface. When you're playing someone whose timing becomes confused, and who can't seem to handle the slice return, stay with it as long as you can. When your opponent begins to start handling it, then go back to your backhand drive or begin mixing them to keep that opponent confused and off balance.

Another time to bring your slice into play is when your opponent is a hit and miss player. The best way to beat him is by keeping the ball *in play* and *in the court*. Eventually, that type of opponent will beat himself by missing returns. A deft combination of drives and slices will mix him up and gain you important points.

Fundamentals of the Slice

Although you must continue the basic one-two-three-four count system, there are some bodily variations between the slice and the drive.

First of all, on Count One (backswing) always take the racket head up higher than your wrist before you begin to move it back. The racket head is more open.

Secondly, on Count Two (step) the racket head goes back farther and is facing the sky but still remains above your wrist.

Third, on Count Three (hit) when the racket head starts forward, it should be either parallel to the ball or *above* it—not below it and moving up as with the drive.

The racket head moves when your arm literally throws it forward and away from your body. The racket head actually moves in a downward forward flight at the oncoming ball. At the moment of contact, the face of the racket closes a little

GROUND STROKES 15

Backhand Slice Hit

Backhand Slice Follow Through

depending upon how much slice you want. The more slice you need or want, the more open your racket should be. Practice the angles of the racket face until you can master the amount of slice you desire for each situation.

On Count Four (follow through) the bottom edge of your racket head is still out ahead of the top edge and leads it all the way through to the finish of the follow through, putting a *slice* on the ball. At the finish of the slice follow through, the racket is generally about head high. If you put a great deal of slice on the ball, it can end up higher.

Unlike the drive, your hitting arm and your right shoulder *do not open up* or roll over. You should be able to see the back of your hand on the slice follow through instead of the palm you see on the drive follow through.

Make sure you get the *feel* of the ball and that you stay with it for that critical six inches of control. Also make sure your arm is completely straight after staying with the ball and all the way through to completion of the follow through.

Your head never lifts on the backhand slice, as it finally does on the drive. Instead, it stays parallel to the ground, forward and out in front of your body.

Finally, on the backhand slice follow through, when you're handling high balls, hop a little bit forward and land on the same front leg. This helps your balance, prepares you for the return, and gives you additional power and control.

BASSETTIP: *Freeze at the end of your slice follow through and check the position of your head. It should not have lifted. Also check the position of your racket hand. You should be able to see the back of it.*

PASSING SHOTS

The passing shot, properly defined, is a

shot that *passes* your opponent when he's at the net or puts that opponent in a bad position to return it, not because he muffed it but because you planned and played it that way. When you learn and master this stroke, you'll be able to get the ball past the net man in doubles and the net rusher or volleyer in singles. If you *don't* learn it, your opponents are going to play the net and pick off your returns, slamming them where you *ain't* for quick and easy points, sets, and matches. It can be a tough shot to play properly because you're usually on the run and don't have the time for perfect form. In fact, within a few seconds you have to get to the ball, utilize the one-two-three-four system that I'll describe, and even decide which *type* of passing shot to use. In addition, you need to hit the passing shot harder than a regular ground stroke and usually with more top spin. Don't panic. Millions of tennis players have developed good passing shots, and you can too. The reward for learning and using this kind of shot effectively can make all the difference between playing hit-and-miss tennis or becoming a consistent winner.

There are some important differences between the forehand and backhand basic strokes and the passing shot. The main difference is that this shot is not intended as an ordinary return but as a strategic type of shot calculated to win a point or at least put your opponent in a poor position to return it. Learn the following differences plus the variations on the basic one-two-three-four count, and you're well on your way to "passing" with flying colors.

First of all, to get the ball past the net man or to get him out of position, you should hit the ball when it is higher off the ground than regular ground strokes. This gives you more speed and robs your opponent of some of the time he needs to get to your return. To hit the ball at a higher location, move up closer to the baseline when your opponent begins volleying. This moves you closer to the ball and lets you contact it at a higher point.

TYPES OF PASSING SHOTS

There are basically three types of passing shots; down-the-line, hard-hit crosscourt, and low, short crosscourt. The down-the-line shot should be hit with little top spin and a great deal of power. The idea is to get this shot by the net man before he can get a racket on it. The faster and deeper you can hit this type of passing shot the better, because you deprive your opponent of the chance of returning it. The second type, or hard-hit crosscourt, is used when the net man or volleyer starts getting your down-the-line shots. You can also use it effectively when the crosscourt is open and unprotected. The third passing shot—the low, short crosscourt—is hit with a great deal of top spin if you're using your forehand and with the back slice (see Chapter 2) if you're using your backhand. Ideally, this return goes back crisply but short and low, forcing the net man to reach for the ball and make a bad volley that you can easily put away. This shot is intended as a strategic change of pace and is aimed at catching your opponent unprepared. This is not strictly a *passing shot* because it usually doesn't *pass* the net man, but it usually does end in a point for you.

I believe that roughly two-thirds of your passing shots should be those hard down-the-line blasts. Even if the shot doesn't get completely by the net man, he has less chance of putting it away for a point. Also, hitting a down-the-line shot while you're on the run is easier than hitting crosscourt.

HIT TOP SPIN

To make your passing shot work properly you need more top spin than you might use on other shots. This increased top spin will cause the ball to dip and drop suddenly as it crosses the net. It's hard for your opponent to follow it with his eyes and his racket. Trying to get it, he will then have to volley upwards and will miss it or set up a weak volley, which you can then put away for a point. But that can work both ways. If *you* don't hit an effective top spin on the ball, you're giving your opponent a high easy volley and probably an easy point.

BASSETTIP: *Remember that the net is higher near the side lines than in the center. Learn to compensate for this difference when hitting the down-the-line shot.*

CANNONBALL

There is one more type of passing shot that is favored by advanced and tournament players. One of my team players calls it a "fuzz lunch" because the ball is hit very hard and very directly at the net man. "If he doesn't get out of the way he'll be wearing a Wilson for a nose," another commented. Actually, both are wrong in the placement. Properly hit, this hard return should be aimed at the opponent's right hip is he is a right hander, left hip if he is a southpaw. By placing the ball at this location, you actually "handcuff" that opponent and prevent a forehand or backhand volley return. There is no practical way the racket can be positioned to pick a ball off the front of the hip.

There is one more type of passing shot—the offensive lob. Because of its strategic importance to your game, I cover it in more detail on pages 25-27.

FOOTWORK

Because you're usually running to make a passing shot, *footwork* is as important as racket work. The passing shot must be a better shot than other ground strokes, and you need position and balance to make it come off. If you have time or if you don't have to run very far to hit the passing shot, then your footwork should be the same as for the forehand or backhand ground stroke. When you're running, get there as fast as you can by taking longer strides and staying low so you won't have to take time to reposition your body for the stroke.

When running hard on the forehand side, hit in an open position more, and hit off the right leg more. This helps you get back into the court faster. Players on clay courts especially like the open position since they can slide into the ball easier. The backhand return of the passing shot doesn't pose the same problem since your coiled body has a more naturally balanced position, even while running.

BASSETTIP: *Make sure your feet stay under your body when running for any shot. If you're off-balance when you hit the shot, that return will be off balance and generally, out of control when it leaves your racket.*

BASSETT SYSTEM FOR PASSING SHOTS

Fundamentally, you use the basic forehand or backhand stroke technique incorporating the following changes.

Count One: Backswing

Because you are going to try hitting the ball harder and at a higher position off the ground, take your racket back higher and farther than the position you use for other ground strokes. Make sure you get that racket backswing started as soon as you see the ball leave the opponent's racket and you have an idea whether you're going to need a forehand or backhand. Remember on the forehand to keep your left hand pointing out and your head low, eyes level with the oncoming ball.

18 TENNIS: THE BASSETT SYSTEM

Backswing for Forehand Passing Shot

Step for Forehand Passing Shot

Backswing for Backhand Passing Shot

Step for Backhand Passing Shot

GROUND STROKES 19

Hit for Forehand Passing Shot

Hit for Backhand Passing Shot

Count Two: Step

As you run down the ball, try to step into it with your front leg, if possible. As you step forward to meet the ball, make sure your racket is back far enough to hit the ball hard but not so far back that you are out of control. Remember, when on the run, hit the forehand off the right leg.

Count Three: Hit

After your step, start uncoiling the racket by throwing the head out and toward the ball. Because you're going to connect with the ball at a high spot off the ground, you don't have to hit *up* on the ball as much to lift it over the net. Make sure you move out rapidly to attack the ball instead of letting it come to you. When you aggressively attack the ball, you develop a positive feeling of control. Waiting for the ball to come to you builds a negative feeling. I have seen fine players lose matches they should have won simply because they were waiting for their opponents shots instead of attacking them.

Count Four: Follow Through

Hold your racket-ball contact for six inches to a foot when you start your follow through. During this *stay* period, your racket head moves in the direction you want the ball to go. After the ball leaves the racket head, your arm should be straight. It moves past the intended line of flight as your shoulder comes forward to touch your chin. If you used top spin, then the arm should end up a little bent and the racket in an end position that is higher than usual.

BASSETTIPS ON PERSONAL STRATEGY

Everyone plays the passing shot differently, based upon experience, natural ability, and training.

Follow Through for Forehand Passing Shot

Follow Through for Backhand Passing Shot

Before trying to do it all, take into consideration what you realistically can do. "Showboating" or trying for great shots you know you can't make only leads to disappointment, lost games, and a general erosion of self confidence. Instead of trying to "kill" your opponent with one fantastic passing shot, stay with the shots you can handle. Let him make the mistakes and give you the points.

Don't be intimidated by the net man in doubles or your singles opponent coming to the net. Many players try to psych you out by coming up, assuming you will panic and make mistakes. Too often, they're right. Instead of watching the opponent, watch the ball and play your own shot. If you don't panic and if you don't try to put the ball away each time you stroke it, you'll get a better than fair share of points.

When a very steady player comes up to the net against you, make that player volley again and again and you should eventually get the point. For some reason, most steady players don't volley very well. If you continue getting the ball back to them, they'll sooner or later make a mistake.

On the other hand, if you're up against a superb volleyer, then your only chance of victory is an effective group of passing shots.

LOBS

The lob can be one of the secret weapons of winning tennis, but many players, even advanced ones, mistakenly believe it's a last ditch desperation shot for the rank (not ranked) amateur. For example, you can throw your opponent completely off his game by lobbing a great deal at the start of a match. High, deep lobs, cleverly mixed with your other ground strokes, should keep him scurrying back from the net and finally will con-

GROUND STROKES 21

Backswing and Step for Forehand Defensive Lob

Backswing and Step for Backhand Defensive Lob

fuse and discourage his net volleying game.

There are two basic types of lobs: the defensive and the offensive. Because they are somewhat different there are two sets of rules and even two different one-two-three-four count methods. Learn them both and practice them as regularly as your other strokes. One other point, don't let the terminology fool you. The offensive lob can be hit when you're desperately trying to retrieve the ball and the defensive lob can be used when you're all set and could have used another type of ground stroke. We'll get into all of that later in this chapter. First, let's look at the variations in the one-two-three-four count which makes up this often overlooked but highly effective stroke. Remember, use your basic ground stroke techniques but with the following changes.

BASSETT SYSTEM FOR DEFENSIVE LOBS

Count One: Backswing

The defensive lob is most often used to save a point you might otherwise lose. Your opponent has hit a well-placed return and your only chance to recover is to keep the ball in the court and in play. To do that, you have to start moving extra fast when you see the ball leave your opponent's racket. Get *your* racket *low* and as far back as possible because the defensive lob needs power to place it both high and deep. Run low to the ground so that your racket can get under the ball. Use long, fast steps, and run toward the *side* of the court *away* from the net to give yourself more time to run down the ball.

Count Two: Step

When you're running to the forehand

Hit for Forehand Defensive Lob

Step and Hit for Backhand Defensive Lob

side, it's almost impossible to hit your return off the front leg. Instead, step back onto your back leg. This helps you get low and under the ball and also keeps you moving away from the net to get more time for your return. An extra second or two can even be gained by letting your body fall back over that back leg and give with the ball as you begin your swing.

On the backhand side, you can usually "give" with the ball off your front leg, but you should still fall back away from the net to give yourself more time to get under it.

Count Three: Hit

When you step back, get that racket head totally under the ball before starting your hit. The racket head should come up flat, almost totally horizontal to the ground. Hit the ball at any height you can get it, even scooping it that last inch before it can bounce twice. Straighten your body as you make contact with the ball. This gives you the power you need for arc and depth. If you're making a desperation reach, however, your arm will have to do the work.

The ball is usually hit flat. One exception is when you're reaching for the ball on the backhand side. Here, the slice return might be more effective. Also, when the opponent has smashed an overhead directly at you and you're cramped for swinging room and time, the slice might save the shot.

Count Four: Follow Through

Hit straight up, perpendicular to the ground. Your racket should end up high; higher than any other shot. Continue straightening up while you fall back and away from the net. If you can jump off the ground do it. This gives you extra power for arc and depth on this shot.

Finally, don't try to scramble back into

Follow Through for Forehand Defensive Lob

Follow Through for Backhand Defensive Lob

the court and position until both feet are back on the ground and you have full balance. You have good recovery time because your opponent can't get to the ball until it comes down, and a good high, deep arc can take what seems like a month and a half.

Defensive Lob Strategy

The basic use of the defensive lob is to keep the ball in play and not give your opponent that point. It's a good defense maneuver and is used by the pros and by advanced players to salvage a bad situation. Here are some tips on how you too can do that:

Be sure to aim your lob for the middle of the opponent's court and deep. It's a mistake to try for accurate placement because you're usually scrambling for the shot, and your return can easily go out of the side lines.

Stay away from the defensive lob when the wind is at your back. Those breezes too often carry the ball outside of the court. On the other hand, use it a great deal when the wind is against you. You can smite it a mighty blow, and the wind should still keep it in the court.

Also use the sun. A high, arcing lob is hard for your opponent to follow when the sun is in his eyes. Don't overlook the elements and the weather as helps to your game. Chances are good your opponent won't, either.

The higher and deeper you hit the ball, the more your opponent might have to wait for it to bounce. While he's waiting you have plenty of time to get back into the court and ready for his return. Also, remember that the deeper you hit the lob, the farther back from the net he has to move to play it.

Because the lob is a slow, time-consuming stroke, this change of pace can often unnerve your opponent, espe-

24 TENNIS: THE BASSETT SYSTEM

Backswing for Forehand Offensive Lob

Step for Forehand Offensive Lob

Backswing for Backhand Offensive Lob

Step for Backhand Offensive Lob

cially if he's the fast reflex type of player. Given time to think about a shot, many of these players will tense up and miss it.

Use the lob to discourage your opponent. No player can stay enthusiastic if his returns are consistently chased down and lobbed back. A sort of psychological weariness will set in eventually, and he'll start missing.

In addition, the lob is a good way to wear your opponent down physically. The overhead smash is a tiring, wearing shot and a series of high lobs will have the same effect on him as body punches do on a boxer.

BASSETT SYSTEM FOR OFFENSIVE LOBS

Okay, that's the defensive lob. Now, let's see how the offensive lob differs from it in stroke production and in strategy.

Count One: Backswing

If you're going for a forehand offensive lob, take your racket back exactly the way you do for a passing shot. For a backhand lob, take the racket back as though you're going to slice. Keep your backswing short so you stay balanced as you run and can get to the ball without reaching.

Count Two: Step

This count is the most important of the four because it's here that you outfox your opponent. Act as though you're going to hit a passing shot. That's what he expects. What he gets is something else, and what you might get is not only a saved play but a point.

You mislead your opponent with body attitudes. When you step into the shot, exaggerate that step. Coil your body as though for a mighty shot. Keep your head down. If you lift it too soon, he'll know you're going to lob. This type of faking should cause a good, experienced opponent to move forward to intercept that ex-

Hit for Forehand Offensive Lob

Hit for Backhand Offensive Lob

Follow Through for Forehand Offensive Lob

Follow Through for Backhand Offensive Lob

pected volley. One caution: Don't so overdramatize that you can't get off an effective lob and end up out-faking yourself instead of him.

Count Three: Hit

The idea of the offensive lob is to get the ball over the head and racket reach of the person you're playing, but *just over*. A higher ball gives him time to retreat and retrieve. To get this *quick*, controlled lob, use top spin on your forehand and even on the backhand if you're good enough to control it on that side. If you're not, use backspin for the backhand lob. Hit the ball a little farther underneath than you would a passing shot. The combination of where and how the racket hits the ball gives you the height and control needed for a successful offensive lob.

BASSETTIP: *Because you're hitting a lob there is a tendency to raise your head to give the ball more top spin and more lift. Fight that urge. A head down attitude will mislead your opponent, and the opposite will give him warning. In this particular case, "heads-up play" doesn't mean smart tennis.*

Count Four: Follow Through

Don't pull up too soon. Try to stay with the ball for a few inches to give your shot deception and control. Swing the racket so it finishes a little higher than the final position for a passing shot. On the forehand, the racket should end up more closed because of the top spin. For the backhand, it finishes more open, because of the slice you put on the ball.

Don't hold this follow through very long because you have to get back into the court to prepare for two possibilities: One, if you didn't hit the shot very well you've given your opponent an easy overhead return; two, even if you did hit it well, he might still get to and return it. If the ball *does* get over his head, get up to the net fast and be ready for any type of return—even including an offensive lob aimed at you.

BASSETTIP: *If you lift your head and body too soon, nothing good can come of it. Your opponent will know a lob is coming and can get ready for it.*

Offensive Lob Strategy

The offensive lob is a strong answer to someone who tries to control the net or who easily picks off your passing shots. It can be effective at other times, too. At a time when your opponent has made a great shot from his back court and put you in trouble, a lob to *his* back court can give you more time to recover and reposition yourself. Also, remember that reflex-type player we talked about in the defensive lob section? He can get impatient, nervous, and off his timing if there's a change of pace created by an offensive lob. That's why you see many excellent players slam lob returns right into the net.

There are three definite times to stay away from the offensive lob. If you have the time and position to hit a passing shot instead of the lob, do it. The percentages are greater that the passing shot will work. Also, never use this shot against a poor player. It's a tough shot and you can lose your own point. Finally, don't use it against a poor volleyer. Force that person to volley by hitting passing shots to him. Eventually the poor volleyer will be poorer by one point.

It's different for a good player. He usually had a good volley. If you find him getting to your passing shots time after time then start throwing up lobs to drive him back from the net. The farther back you can move him, the tougher it is for him to get off a good volley return.

BASSETTIP: *When you start gaining control of your offensive lob, begin placing it to your opponent's backhand. It's extremely hard to put away a high backhand return. You will usually get a soft, somewhat out-of-control return, which you should be able to place for a point.*

APPROACH SHOT

Although underestimated by many players, I like to approach the approach shot with great respect because it (a) gives you controlled return of a ball that's been hit short to you, (b) can often put you in a position to put the ball away for a point, and (c) moves you up into the favorable net and volleying position at a time when your opponent can't hit a passing shot or a lob or catch you in the no man's land of middle court.

Don't make the mistake of counting on the approach shot as a consistent winner, however. Some players do and are already congratulating themselves as the opponent's return comes whipping by them.

The approach shot is played differently—in stroke production and in strategy—than other shots and the differences should be learned in order to have an effective one.

You usually hit this shot while you're running forward. Your racket should contact the ball at a height somewhere between your waist and your shoulders, considerably higher than most ground strokes. Hitting it there gives you two advantages: Your chances of putting the ball into the net go way down, and you get the ball back to your opponent faster, many times rushing him into making a mistake.

On *forehand* approach shots hit the ball hard and fairly flat for depth, adding a touch of top spin for control. If you're scooping up a low ball, add more top spin to lift it over the net. As you know from an earlier chapter, I don't agree with slice forehands. One exception is the low approach shot when you're running hard and you're desperate to save the point.

Backswing for Forehand Approach Shot

Backswing for Backhand Approach Shot

Here, try a slice as a last ditch effort. When you do have time, however, play the shot properly.

It's different for the *backhand* approach shot. Here, especially when you're running hard to the ball, the slice becomes your strongest angle of racket attack to make the approach shot work. The only exception might be if you're meeting the ball at a height above the net, then you should flat-drive it. Otherwise, the backhand slice helps you get the shot off faster, and helps you get to the net faster when hitting on the run.

Forehand approach shots should be aimed down the line most of the time. When you go to the *backhand* approach for this shot, you can hit wherever you feel comfortable. A down-the-line approach has the advantage of staying low (because of the slice), but it has the disadvantage of going to his forehand, which could be his strongest stroke. If you go to the cross-court return, smack it deep—deeper than the down-the-line return so he can't step into it with maximum power and control.

BASSETT SYSTEM FOR THE APPROACH SHOT

Count One: Backswing

Start rushing up to meet the ball when you realize it's going to come in short. Get your racket into a short high backswing instantly. Because you're going to hit the ball at a higher point than you do most shots, the racket should go back and stay back at a higher point. A long backswing will throw you off balance and hobble your run. While you're running, hold the racket with only *one* hand, using the other to help you keep balance as you rush forward.

Face the ball and the net as you run toward them. Use long steps to cover ground rapidly, but as you get closer to the ball, shorten them to give yourself

Step for Forehand Approach Shot

Step for Backhand Approach Shot

maximum balance. Once again, your body should be low, head out in front of your feet, and eyes low and level to the ball.

When you get close to the ball, move the free hand to the shaft of the racket. On the forehand just touch the racket before taking it back farther. On the backhand actually use the free hand to help complete the backswing, and don't let go until you start the racket forward to meet the ball.

Count Two: Step

When you're running into the approach shot and want to continue on to the net, the step is different than the one you take for other ground strokes.

For the *forehand* make your step forward, and then push off from your right (back) leg. This helps you run right through the ball while keeping your balance.

For the *backhand* there are two optional steps. With the first, you step into your right (front) leg, hit the ball, and then hop forward on that same leg. This step seems to work best for *high* approaches and those that you hit down the line. In the second step, you step forward with your left leg and then hit off it. This keeps you moving rapidly into the net and seems to work best for *low* approach shots. Practice both of these steps to find out which is the most comfortable and effective for you.

Count Three: Hit

Because you're running, make sure to throw your racket head out to meet the ball while it is still in front of you. Don't run through the ball and hit it late! The best way to avoid this is to make sure your head and shoulders are leaning out in front of your legs and feet, your head at eye level to the ball and parallel to the

30 TENNIS: THE BASSETT SYSTEM

Hit for Forehand Approach Shot

Follow Through for Forehand Approach Shot

Hit for Backhand Approach Shot

Follow Through for Backhand Approach Shot

ground during the entire stroke. Your swing should stay parallel to the ground and the racket should meet the ball at a height above the waist, or better yet, at chest or shoulder height.

Count Four: Follow Through

Keep your racket in contact with the ball after you hit it; then follow through as if you'd hit a ground stroke. Also, keep your body leaning forward while you run toward the net. Don't pull up, away from the shot, and don't look to see where the ball is going too soon. When you slice the backhand approach shot, your head and right shoulder should lean in the direction you want the ball to go, and they actually aim it there.

FOOTWORK

After you hit the ball, lengthen your stride again to get to your net position fast; then get set just before your opponent hits his passing shot. If your shot went down the middle, then take the middle of the net. If it went down either side, take that side.

APPROACH SHOT STRATEGY

A surprising number of approach shots can be sure putaways if you get good depth on them. Keep trying to read your opponent to spot his weaknesses, and then take advantage of them.

If you've spotted a weak forehand or backhand in your opponent, hit the approach shot to that side. Some players can't handle spins very well. Hit the ball with back spin, which keeps it low, or with top spin, which makes the ball jump erratically after it bounces.

If you're playing someone who moves well, don't necessarily hit your approach to the open court. Many times, you can get the point by hitting the ball *behind* him, especially if you can catch that player on the wrong foot or going the wrong way. If he is slow in covering court, then definitely place it in the open area.

Change pace for some players, especially the fast-relax type. Now and then float a slow, easy, high approach to upset his timing and perhaps psych him into making a mistake.

One of the most effective strategies is also one of the simplest. Hit your approach shot down the middle of the court. Your opponent has to take time to decide between a forehand or a backhand return, and in that momentary confusion he can even get "handcuffed." Also, it's hard to get a good angle on a passing return when it comes down the middle.

DROP SHOT

This shot has a lot going for it. It can be a dependable point-getter against a lot of players. It can pull even the best players out of position. And it also gives you a chance to prove what a fine professional actor you could be.

There are two requirements for the drop shot: The ball should be coming to you slow and short so it will land around the service line area; and your opponent should be deep in his own court, preferably behind his baseline. (Don't use the drop shot on a slow, *high* ball. Use your approach shot instead.) Hit the ball softly, gently and with back spin so it will stop when it hits the ground. Follow through a few inches to feel the back spin taking hold. The ball should just clear the net so your opponent hasn't time to cover it. If you pop up, it's too easy for him to get to the ball and smash it away from you.

The drop shot is perfect for faking out the other guy because you can attack it exactly like an approach shot and as he gets set for that, you place the ball where it's least expected. To do this, use the approach shot backswing and act, act, act

32 TENNIS: THE BASSETT SYSTEM

Backswing and Step for Forehand Drop Shot

Hit for Forehand Drop Shot

Backswing and Step for Backhand Drop Shot

Hit for Backhand Drop Shot

GROUND STROKES   33

Follow Through for Forehand Drop Shot

Follow Through for Backhand Drop Shot

like you're going to whack it a mighty blow. This theatrical performance is easier on the backhand side because you hit the drop shot just the way you slice. Although the racket head is also up for the forehand side, deception seems to be tougher.

This is an important shot so it's important to practice it. College team players use drills you can easily do and that can give you mastery of this shot. Get someone to practice with you. Let the ball bounce once on your side, and then hit it easy, low, and just over the net, using a lot of back spin. You can go either down the line or crosscourt, just so it barely clears the net. Try to run your practice partner from side to side, and have him do the same to you. This workout will develop your touch, shot angles, placement, and general overall conditioning. You can add interest to it by playing points.

As you get good at it, make it a little tougher by using only the service courts as the playing area. Any ball deeper than the service line is out. You can even tighten up on this drill by restricting yourselves to one service court on each side of the net.

One warning about the drop shot: Even if you've learned the shot and can control it, don't begin depending upon it too often. I once had a fine team player who could hit picture-book drop shots and did even when he was off balance or out of position. It didn't take his opponents long to begin expecting them and setting up returns for which he wasn't prepared. His game fell off and so did his value to the team until he backed off those drop shots and began to redevelop his all around game. He learned (and you should too) not to depend upon the drop shot too much. Use this shot only when the situation warrants it.

DROP SHOT STRATEGY

Like most other strokes, every time you

hit a drop shot you must decide whether to hit it down the line or crosscourt. If you want to get the ball over the net fast, go down the line because the ball doesn't have to go as far. But, your opponent doesn't have as far to run either. If your down the line isn't hit well, a good opponent can run it down and has an easy put away. To put the ball down the line, just block it instead of trying to get the racket head around to angle the ball crosscourt. If your opponent does manage to get to your down-the-line drop shots, he is in very bad shape for your lob.

Hitting the drop shot crosscourt pulls your opponent out of position so you can put away your next return. This shot has farther to travel, but your opponent has farther to run because he has to move both up *and* across to reach it. I like to use the crosscourt against fast players because it does force them to move out of their court where I can place the next shot. I also think it's safer because the ball doesn't have to land so close to the net and still remain unreachable or unplayable. Down the line seems to work best against slower players.

When you get that opponent fast enough to reach and return a well-hit crosscourt drop shot, try a ground stroke or volley immediately to the open court, and you should have another point.

The drop shot, especially the down-the-line shot, can set up depth perception problems for the receiver. Most players can estimate the depth of a shot when it angles across the net but have difficulty judging how deep a down-the-line shot is going to come into his court. He often misjudges its shallowness, and this gives him a late start getting to the ball. One of the toughest opponents is the steady hitter who prefers ground strokes over volleys. The secret here is play a waiting, patient game until he hits a short ball and then return either a drop shot or an approach shot. Although you should mix them up, the drop shot brings him up into a part of the court he isn't used to playing in. He'll be uncomfortable, unsure of himself, and eventually should blow the point.

BASSETTIP: *Most players run left or right adequately but don't run up and back very much when they play tennis. Whenever you get a chance to mislead your opponent's depth perception, do it with short down-the-line drop shots.*

TWO-HANDED STROKE

Along with day-glo colored balls, metal rackets, and pastel court clothes, the two-handed stroke is becoming more popular in today's tennis. The stroke has actually been around for a long time. The great Pancho Segura dominated men's tennis for years with his fearsome doublehanded forehand. Today, Jimmy Connors, Chris Evert, and other two-handed stars are on the TV tube almost as much as a Tide commercial, and their hitting techniques are being copied by players throughout the world. Because this technique is becoming increasingly important to a growing number of new and even experienced players, I wanted to devote a chapter to its advantages, disadvantages, and the proper and improper ways to play a two-handed forehand, backhand, or both.

Not everyone can play a two-handed stroke. There are two necessary qualities to make it come off. Because it is a tiring, wearing method, you must be in very good physical condition; and because you do not get as much reach on the shot, you must be very quick on your feet. Even if you are strong and fast, you should know the problems before experimenting with the two-handed shot.

DISADVANTAGES

With today's fast courts, speedy balls, and tightly strung rackets, the game is becoming increasingly speedier. It's tough enough to make some return shots using a one-handed stroke, and the sad fact is, that the two-handed stroke takes more time. If you have the time to get set, then the two-handed shot can be highly effective. If you don't, then you're putting yourself at a disadvantage using this stroke. The two-handed shot is especially difficult to pull off when you're running fast and have to reach for the ball (which is a great deal of the time in most matches). It's doubly bad on the backhand side because your legs begin to tangle up, and you can't use your free arm to keep balance.

More than a few players get confused hitting ground strokes two handed but volleys with one hand. The two-handed volley isn't as effective as the one-handed because your reach is limited. Since there is no consistency (two hands on some strokes, one hand on others), these players become mixed up, confused, and end up with neither a good two-handed or even one-handed game.

On the important backhand side, the one-handed volley, half volley, low approach shot, and ground strokes can be affected badly by changing to a two-handed ground stroke because of grip changes. Remembering which grip, when, and where, while trying to get to a bulletlike ball can throw off the game of even the most organized of minds.

ADVANTAGES

To offset these disadvantages, there are several major advantages that go along with a two-handed game.

The first game most of us learn is baseball or stick ball and its two-handed swing. When we discover tennis, the natural tendency is to swing the "bat" the same way. This feels good to young players because it gives them control, and most importantly, it gives them power to get the ball over the net. Nothing will drive a ten year old back to Little League faster than not even being able to get the ball to his opponent. So, the two-handed stroke has a definite advantage for the young, the small, or the not too strong.

In addition, you can use more deception with two-handed strokes. Your racket moves faster, so you can wait until the last second before hitting the ball. Your opponent not only can't recognize your return shot but many times can't even see it come off your racket until it is too late. This gives you a major advantage for drop shots, lobs, passing shots and return of serves.

The two-handed shot is also a godsend for those players who have a tendency toward that annoying disability known as *tennis elbow*. It puts much less stress on that sensitive joint and has helped half-crippled players return to a full and winning game.

The two-handed grip keeps the racket steady, even for players whose hands sweat a lot. And, last, the two-handed stroke can become the *big shot* for players who don't have one. There are literally millions of players who have a balanced game but no single big stroke they can count on for sure points. Because of its power and control, the two-handed shot could provide this winning margin for many of them.

After reviewing these pros and cons, if you're still intrigued with the idea, here's how the two-handed strokes are manufactured.

BASSET SYSTEM FOR THE TWO-HANDED FOREHAND STROKE

The grip is different. Learn it or your two-handed stroke will not work. Start by holding the racket in an ordinary forehand grip, but *move your hand up the handle* a few inches. This makes way for your left hand to grab the bottom of the

Backswing for Two-Handed Forehand Stroke

Step for Two-Handed Forehand Stroke

handle. The major problem you'll find here comes when you want a two-handed forehand and a one-handed backhand. When you go to your backhand, you must not only change your grip but have to get your hand back to the bottom of the shaft again. Doing both can take extra time, time that can make the difference between a hit and a miss.

Count One: Backswing

When you're running for the ball, don't ever use two hands on your backswing. Take your racket back one handed and use the other arm to keep yourself on balance and in fast motion toward the interception point. Only when you're ready to start your step into the ball do you grab the racket with the left hand. Doing it too soon (or too late) destroys the rhythm and power of the two-handed shot. One bonus of this technique is that your backswing stays in control because the second hand keeps it from going back too far. Since the racket isn't too far back, this also allows you to go into the circular-type backswing for more power.

Count Two: Step

Just before stepping into the ball that second hand should grab the bottom of the racket handle. Because your left arm is reaching over, your body will go into a more tightly coiled position, almost totally closed. Tighten that coil by turning your forward (or left) shoulder even more away from the net, to the right, by turning your knees. Then drop the left shoulder down close to the ball and pull your head down.

Count Three: Hit

Keep your elbows in as you uncoil your body to hit the ball. Use your shoulders for power as you swivel to connect, then let the elbows move out a bit away from

Hit for Two-Handed Forehand Stroke

Follow Through for Two-Handed Forehand Stroke

the body at the moment of contact. Another bonus of the two-handed forehand is that you don't have to watch the position of your head as much as you do with the one-handed shot. The two hands tend to keep it down and steady, exactly where you want it.

Count Four: Follow Through

As with the one-handed forehand, stay with the ball from six to twelve inches after you meet it. If you're looking for top spin, bring the racket head up high and close to your head with the elbows bent. If you want power and depth instead, move the racket out toward the ball and finish with your arms straight.

Because your body is uncoiling you'll feel like jumping up after you hit the ball to give the hit more power. This can be good providing you (a) stay with the ball through the stroke and (b) that you jump *forward* as well as up. Jumping straight up can pull the racket away from the ball.

Most two-handed players end up with both hands on the racket all the way. Letting go too soon with the second hand can throw off your stroke.

BASSETT SYSTEM FOR THE TWO-HANDED BACKHAND STROKE

Unlike the one-handed backhand, you *do not change grips* on the two-handed stroke. Use the forehand grip. Your right hand (once again, left-handed players are asked to transpose these instructions) should grip the racket at the bottom of the handle while the left hand goes on top of that.

Count One: Backswing

Once again, get your racket back fast. If you have a long way to run, hold it with only one hand while you're gliding across the court. If you don't have far to move, use your other hand right away, grabbing

Backswing for Two-Handed Backhand Stroke

Step for Two-Handed Backhand Stroke

the racket with your left hand six to ten inches above the right or about where you'd "balance" the racket for a one-handed shot.

Take the racket straight back in a short and controlled swing. The right arm will keep it from going back too far. In addition, your right shoulder will come down low and pull your head down low. Get down to the ball, not by bending your back, but using your knees to control the up and down motion. Just before you step into the ball, bring your left hand down next to the right hand. This will help your rhythm.

Count Two: Step

Step forward into the ball shifting your weight onto your right leg. Plant your foot more to the left than you would for the one-handed shot. This helps you keep balance when both arms are into your body. Coil your body to a tightly closed position, swinging your right shoulder around to the left. Keep your arms straight and move the racket back as far as it will go comfortably. It can't overswing.

Count Three: Hit

Move your shoulder forward and throw your racket head up and out, away from your body to meet the ball. Your shoulders and arms give you power for this hit and your legs also help as you straighten your knees. When you hit the ball, move your arms away from your body until the left arm is totally straight and the right one bent just a bit. Try to hit *under* the middle of the ball to get the most top spin.

Count Four: Follow Through

As with all shots, stay with the ball at least six inches. After that there are several ways you can finish the stroke, all good

Hit for Two-Handed Backhand Stroke

Follow Through for Two-Handed Backhand Stroke

depending upon your particular abilities and likes or dislikes.

Some players like Billy Martin let go of the racket with the left hand right after hitting the ball. Billy feels that he can not only get ready faster for the next shot, but it helps him keep his balance. Other players hold onto the racket with both hands all the way through the stroke, and some even bring the racket back to the ready position with both hands still on the handle.

Jimmy Connors ends his two-handed backhand by throwing the racket head out after the ball. This gives him more depth. Harold Solomon pulls his racket head up close to his head after he has hit the ball. This adds more top spin to his hit and also confuses his opponents.

Those are some variations of championship tennis players. For most others, I recommend you finish with the left arm straight, the right arm bent, the racket head high, and the body facing the net. Most intermediate and beginning players should not leave the ground to gain more power on this stroke. You might see world tennis stars do it on television, but they've already mastered their control and balance and ability to get ready for the next return.

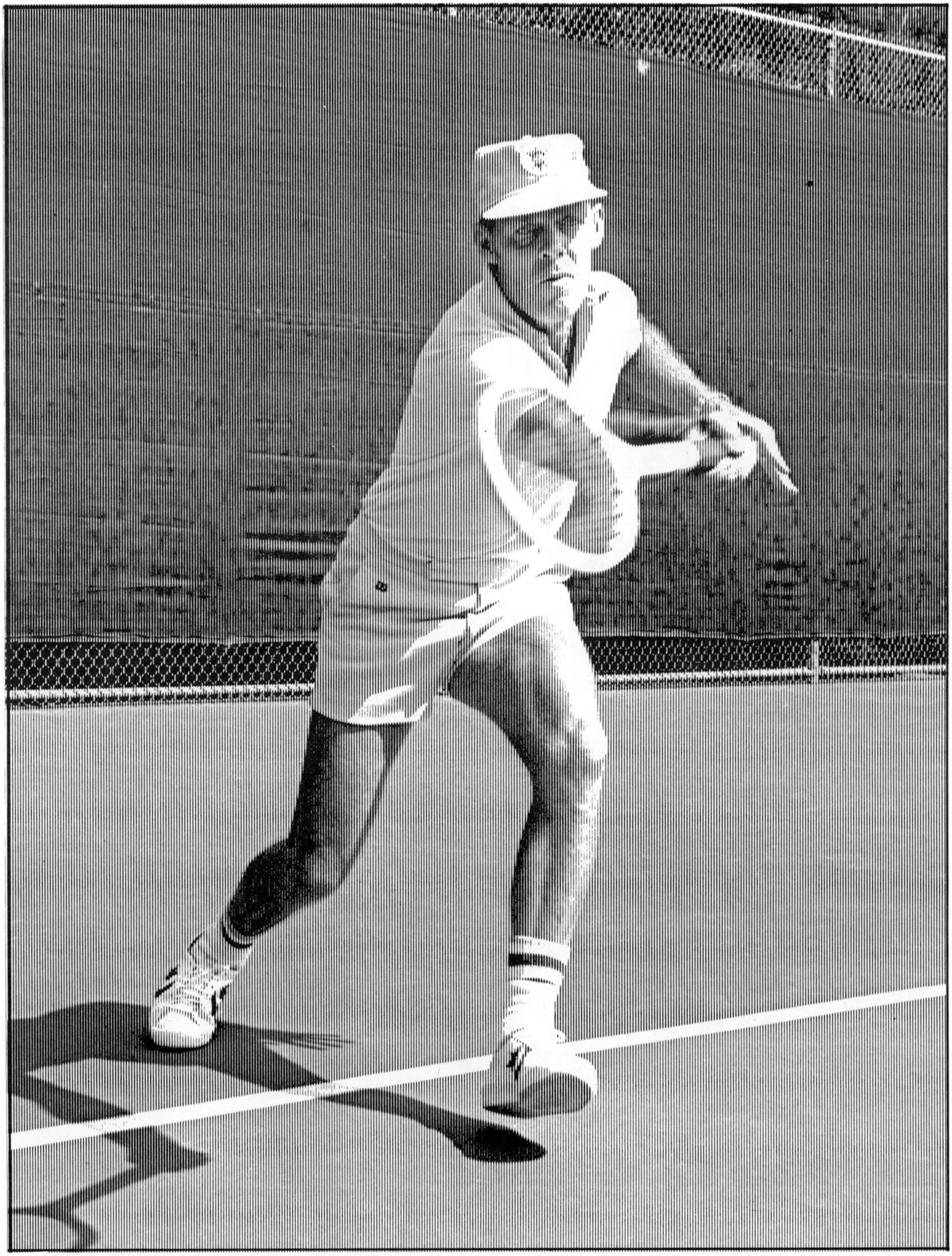

2. Serves

On a scale of one to ten the importance of your serve would rate a fifteen. No other single stroke in the game of tennis gives you so many advantages, so much control of the game, and so many opportunities to score points. If you develop a good serve, chances are you'll develop a good, winning game. If you don't, you can't. I don't know any other way of saying it. Consider the advantages of a good serve:

- You have total control of the ball. You are acting upon your opponent's game not reacting to it.
- You have the psychological advantage of being on the attack, putting your opponent on the defensive.
- You can win points without tiresome running, chasing, and wearing yourself out.
- You can compensate for weakness in the rest of your game.

But, if you don't develop your serve:

- You can lose points and games faster with a bad serve than with any other undeveloped stroke, by double faulting.
- You can lose points and games by giving your opponent easy setups and returns that he can put away for points.
- You can psych yourself and become discouraged, throwing off the rest of your game.

You've probably noticed that every open, tournament, or professional tennis player has either a big, fast serve or a cunning, tricky one. Most have both. All have control of their serves, or I guarantee you, they couldn't have come as far in competition tennis as they have. You've also probably noticed that size and strength have little to do with an effective service. The smaller Rod Laver of the tennis world can very often out-serve the bigger, stronger John Newcombes and Stan Smiths. Small women players, ten year olds, even grandmothers can all have a wicked, point-winning serve once they learn it. Because there's a lot going on all at once it's not the easiest stroke to master right away, but it is definitely, definitely the most essential one to master. Let's start with the correct way to hold the racket:

GRIP

There are two. You can use the standard eastern forehand grip or that modified backhand grip called the continental. The forehand grip gives you a fast bullet-type serve. Some players use it only on the first serve while others use it for both first and second. The continental grip sacrifices speed but gives you more spin and more control of the ball. A great many players use this grip for both serves to gain accurate placement of the ball and to give the ball the spin that throws off an opponent's attempted return.

STANCE

If you don't stand correctly you can't serve correctly. To serve to your opponent's forehand court stand behind your baseline and one or two feet to the right of the center line. This position gives you the best possible angles for placing shallow, angled serves that go out of court before your opponent can reach them or down the line serves which hit exactly on or near the service center line. For the backhand court, move two or three feet to the left of center line.

When you take your stance, put your left foot about an inch behind the baseline and at a forty-five-degree angle so the toe points toward the net post to your right. The right foot should be about shoulder width distance from the left and about parallel to the baseline. If you draw an imag-

Bouncing the Ball for Rhythm

inary line from the right big toe to the left big toe, that line, if continued, would show you where the ball will land in the service court. When your feet are in position, shift weight to the front foot. Take a look at the court to which you're serving. Bounce the ball two, three, or four times, while breathing deeply, relaxing, and concentrating on the serve. This bouncing helps you start the rhythm so important to a good serve. Stretch your right arm and racket back. When you're ready to start your serve, shift the weight back on your right leg and go into your ready position.

READY POSITION

Your front leg should be fairly straight, the back leg slightly bent, your weight sitting comfortably over it and balanced on the balls of your feet. Lean your body out a little to the right as you point the top of the racket at your opponent. Your left

Ready Position for Serve

hand not only holds the balls you're going to serve but cradles the racket at the throat. Remember, you're now creating a rhythm pattern so don't stay in the ready position very long. Look at the spot where you're going to serve for the second time and fix it in your mind.

BASSETT SYSTEM FOR SERVE

Count One: Backswing

For a good, strong backswing both arms must go down together and come up together. Drop your left arm a bit, and then move it up in front of you and to the right. At the same time, drop the right arm down behind you and to the right. Start both arms upward at the same moment, moving your left shoulder forward and to the right. At the same exact moment, shift weight to the front leg, bending that knee a little. (It's important not to pick your left foot off the ground because you're going to have to pivot on it.)

Hold the ball you're going to serve on your left-hand fingertips, the other ball cradled farther back in that hand. As the left hand reaches shoulder height toss the ball up straight—*without spin*. The correct height for your toss is a point where the middle of your strings can meet the ball when your right arm is fully extended upwards. (You can practice the height of your toss by holding your racket straight up against a tennis court fence and noting where the center of the racket comes. Then try tossing the ball to hit that spot again and again and again.) You also place the ball so that if it fell it would land a few inches in front of and to the right of your front foot. From this point on, keep your head up, eyes on the ball, until you finish. After releasing the ball, your hand should stay facing the sky, palm up and pointing to the ball. Remember, earlier we said that right arm not only goes down but comes up with the left arm. When you take your left arm down to start the toss, drop your right arm, putting the racket head below your wrist and close to the ground so you can get a pendulum effect on your upswing. When the left arm lifts, bring the right one up, bending it at the elbow a little when the racket head gets above your shoulder. The correct position here forms a V with the left arm in front of you and the right arm behind you and both above your head.

Count Two: Elbow Bend

This particular count is the most important part of your serve. When you get both arms up and are ready to hit the ball, move your right elbow forward and up, ahead of your arm and toward the net. This bends your arm back toward your shoulder and puts your forearm tightly against the bicep. It also cocks your wrist. You need both the whipping action from your elbow plus the snapping action of your wrist to get off a good, point-

Backswing for Serve

winning serve. When that elbow goes forward, it will automatically force your hand to drop the racket head down in a low, back-scratching position. It's only from here that you can get that sure whipping action behind your serve. If you start the serve with your racket higher, you're depending upon muscle alone, and that isn't enough for a truly strong service game. Start the serve with the elbow action. Only now, after the racket has gone into that dropped position, are you ready to go after the ball with the racket.

Count Three: Hit

Be sure your head stays up all the way through contact with the ball. You can't hit what you can't see. On the first serve time your contact so the racket will meet the ball before it starts dropping. If it drops, it will hit low on your racket and go into the net. On the second serve, however, you can let the ball drop an inch or two because you're generally not hitting as hard and because you want to get a little more spin on the ball. When you hit the ball, use all of that behind the back windup for whipping action and then just before making contact, snap your wrist up and over the ball. The rhythm on this stroke is important. Start your backswing slowly, move the arm up and drop the racket with a little more speed, and then whip rapidly through the hit, without pausing anywhere from start to finish. Some players whisper to themselves, "S-l-o-w, FAST!" as they go through the hit, and I even knew one competition player who used to yell out, "W-o-o-o-oEEEE!" during every serve to give himself the proper timing.

There are two more body movements during the hit. Your left arm will come down naturally as the racket is going up to meet the ball. Your right leg goes up and forward into the air and even with the left leg as you are making contact.

There are three kinds of serves you should learn. They're all good and each is used for a different type of situation, opponent, or game. Most good players mix them up.

FLAT SERVE

This is a power serve with no spin. It travels in a straight line and continues in that line after it bounces. And it can make a strong first serve because you hit the racket flat through the ball. It's usually a low percentage serve, and if it's not working for you, abandon it. However, if it is going in and earning points, stay with it until it weakens, and then switch to another serve. One psychological disadvantage of the fast, hard flat serve is that when it does go in you expect either a weak return or none at all. Should the return come back to you just as fast, you're going to be caught in the back court and may not be able to get cross- or up court fast enough to return it. Its main advantage is a speed that can catch slower opponents just standing there watching you literally "ace" them out.

SLICE

This serve is a left-hander's dream because it "slices" the ball to the backhand side of the opponent in both courts. If you're a southpaw, use it most of the time. For right-handers, this service is best when serving to the forehand court because it can slice off to the right and out of court after it bounces or can squeeze the right-handed receiver when returning his backhand. The major disadvantage is that it's difficult to place the slice exactly into the right-handed receiver's backhand because he can run around it for a forehand return. The slice is also a strong, effective serve when sent to a left-hander because it goes easily to his backhand and away from him. To slice the serve, get your body around faster, faster than for the flat serve. Toss the ball more in front of you and more to the right. Hit the ball on its right half and make sure the racket stays with the ball until it gives it good slice action. A well-hit slice should curve to the left when it leaves your racket and continue curving to the left as it kicks off its bounce.

TOP SPIN

To me this is the best all-around serve for a right-hander because it's controllable and fast; it has variations and is easy to hit into a right-handers backhand. The top-spin serve is hard to return because it's unpredictable, bouncing straight back or to the right of the receiver's right after it hits. To put top spin on the ball, hit it under the left side and then "peel" your racket up and over the top right side, in a left-to-right racket motion. On your first serve toss the ball a little more to the right and a little more in front of you, and

Elbow-Hit for Serve

don't put too much spin on it. If that doesn't go in, then add more spin, or go to variations for your second serve.

Count Four: Follow Through

Make sure your head is still up and your eyes on the ball. After the racket hits the ball, keep it moving in the desired direction for a few inches, and then bring the racket down your right side before crossing your body and finishing at the left. The whipping action of your elbow and snap of your wrist should have that racket head speeding right along by now, so make sure you don't perform open leg surgery with it. In addition to the whip and snap, you also need your entire body behind each serve. To put everything into it, swing your right leg (which should be in the air during the hit) forward so it lands ahead of your left leg at the same time your left leg is swung up and back. This puts your entire body in the air be-

Follow Through for Serve

-hind the serve, and the momentum propels you into the court ready for a deep return or a fast move up to the net. I call this a *fast reverse action* with your feet.

The serve may sound as complicated and disjointed as a new disco dance, but it truly isn't. Like that disco dance, the serve has a definite rhythm to it with different parts of your body working smoothly and harmoniously to create the overall stroke. Learning that rhythm, especially where it speeds up, is absolutely essential to a good serve. Remember, Count One starts off slowly and then Two, Three, and Four speed up. 1---2--3-4 fast! Never, ever, stop or pause between counts. You're trying to develop one continuous motion from backswing until completion of follow through. The most flagrant timing offender is a ball tossed too high. If you have to wait for it to come down, it's going to ruin the rhythm of your serve and affect power, control, and your entire serve.

PRACTICE

Because of its importance, nothing needs more practice than your serve, nothing. Get a bucket of old balls and practice your toss, your backswing, your hit, your follow through, and the three different types of serves. Practice serving to both courts, to imaginary left-handers, right-handers, to forehands, to backhands. Practice first serves, second serves, and variations on the top spin. While you're doing that, also practice your entry into the court. As you finish your follow through, head for the net. Get into the court with long, fast strides, and then go into those small, quick steps to your set position.

Make sure you practice both the serve and the moves to the net at the same time. A lot of players get used to practicing serves without leaving the baseline and then don't leave it even during matches.

After practicing toss, rhythm, and types of serves, then practice "placing" the ball. Give yourself a real target. Put an empty ball can, a tennis bag, a racket cover or even a sweater down in the court where you want the ball to hit. Try again and again to hit that target. When you're getting to it, move it to more difficult angles. Practice hitting targets in both forehand and backhand courts. Start out practicing by yourself, but as you improve have a buddy or partner there to see how well your serve is really coming in and to return the balls. One warning: Don't try to put too much spin or speed on the ball when you first start practicing. You can injure your arm and shoulder. Wait until you're completely warmed up before putting everything into it. Read Chapter 6 on practice.

STRATEGY

A good serve is fifty percent, and knowing what to do with it is the other half.

The serve is a percentage shot. You must reach the stage where a high percentage of your first serves go in; and when they don't, you should be able to place your second serve into the opponent's backhand, where he has less chance of returning it.

Because most opponents expect a weaker second serve, put more power into it every now and then, catching them literally flat-footed and unprepared to return it. However, if you're winning or getting a good percentage of your serves in, don't change what you're doing. Stay with it until the percentages turn against you.

It does no good to deliver a magnificent serve and then miss your opponent's return. This happens quite often, especially to players with a consistently good serve. These players don't expect a return, and when the ball does come back they're not prepared. Always expect a return. If it doesn't come back you haven't lost anything. If it does, you're in position and ready to respond. But don't rush to the net after *every single* serve. Sometimes you should stay back at the baseline. This change of pace can confuse your opponent and also lets you play the basic ground strokes.

Use change of pace on the placement and speed of your serves. Don't serve to the same place with the same speed all the time. Keep your opponent guessing. Mix up serves to forehands and backhands, slow and fast serves, flats, spins, and slices. And remember you're serving *to the court* and not to the opponent. If you watch the other player, his moves and shifts may confuse you and cause double faults. Just look at the spot on the court where you want the ball to go and serve there. Don't let your opponent's hops, jumps, skips, and lunges fool you into serving up exactly the ball he can put away.

RETURN OF SERVE
THE IMPORTANCE OF THE SHOT

Good players today must have a great return of serve. When players were playing on faster courts, the serve and volley game was predominant. You'll notice nowadays that the good players—Jimmy Connors, Chris Evert, Harold Solomon, Borg—are winning with returns of serves and all-around games. The best thing they do is return the serve. When a player returns the serve well, the opponent becomes psychologically flustered. Most players who have their serve go out on them have the rest of the game go out on them too. So the return of the serve makes these players start thinking, "What's wrong with my serve?" And they worry about it so much, that their entire game deteriorates. They don't give you credit for returning the serve well; they just think that they are doing something wrong. The next thing you know their forehand or their volley or their backhand ground strokes start to go just because they have become discouraged with their serve.

THREE TYPES OF RETURNS
Server Stays Back

If the server stays back, there's no need for you to do very much with a return of serve. All you need to do is hit it as a regular ground stroke. You get a little bit farther back behind the baseline than you normally would so that the ball will peak over and come down just as a regular ground stroke. You hit this shot deep with no pressure at all because you know that the server is not coming to the net. The main thing is not to miss this type of return, because if you get it back fairly deep in the court, you've neutralized the other person's serving advantage. Don't try to do too much with this shot. Now, if you hit the ball back to this person's backhand, that's even better. What you don't want to do is hit very short so he can approach on the next shot or put it away on you.

Server Comes In—Weak Volley

If you have a server who comes into the net but who has a weak volley, you should still hit his serve as a regular ground stroke. Don't try to do too much; don't rush it; just hit a normal ground stroke. Now this type of server is probably coming into the net just to intimidate you, hoping that you will miss. But you must get the ball back into play and make him volley. He might hit a few volleys away on you for points, which might frighten you into making better returns. But if you just keep returning the ball steadily and consistently, this person's weak volley will show up. Don't hit and miss. Make him volley. Keep hitting regular ground strokes, keep your eye on the ball, and don't watch the server come in.

Server Comes In—Good Volley

The next type of a return is to a server who comes in and can volley well. Now, this is mainly what we're going to be talking about on the return of serve section. The first thing you have to know about is where you're going to be standing in preparation.

WHERE YOU STAND

Usually you will stand for the first serve about two feet behind the baseline, halfway between where your opponent might serve to your forehand or your backhand. You cannot leave any space open. If the opponent serves mostly to your forehand, you can move a little bit over to the right. If he serves to your backhand most of the time, you can move a little bit over to your left. Most good players will mix it up. They'll serve some to your forehand and some to your backhand. So you have to be halfway between. What you can't let your opponent do is rush you. You must always have your head down until you're ready to make the return shot. Don't let him quick-serve you. Put your hand up if you're not ready to return the serve. Always have the server wait for you. Don't let yourself wait for him or be rushed by him. You must not always stand in the same place. Instead of being two feet back of the baseline for the first serve, sometimes you can stand on the baseline or six or eight feet in back of the baseline. Don't always give him the same perspective. Move around a little bit: up and back and also left and right. Every once in a while on a second serve you can move over a little bit to your left or right. If you stand in the same place all the time and hit the same return, the ball is always going to get back to the server at the same time and then he gets used to making the volley at the same moment all the time. You must change pace and change your position a little bit so he'll be hitting the ball in a different place.

WHEN SERVER TOSSES THE BALL UP

As soon as the server starts to throw the ball up, you must watch that ball even though the server has not hit it yet. You must start getting up on your toes and inching forward a little bit. At this time your head is in front of your body, your shoulders too are leaning forward—not off balance—but definitely leaning forward. You're moving your feet now. You should jump up a little bit off the ground when your opponent actually throws the ball up and inch forward. You're having quick feet.

HIT RETURN ABOUT SHOULDER HIGH

When your opponent hits the serve, you must feel as though you're going out to the ball enough so you can hit the ball shoulder high. That is the spot you want—shoulder high. You want this spot in order to hit the ball out and down at your opponent's feet. You don't have to lift the ball up over the net, and you will get the ball back more quickly. Don't let the ball peak over; you're getting the ball on the rise and hitting it shoulder high. You get the ball back to your opponent before he gets in position to volley. This rushes your opponent. The return of the serve is very much like the volley. You have to go out to *intercept* it. In order to hit the ball at the proper spot you sometimes have to hurry up to meet the ball. You have to get up to it quickly to get it shoulder high. Sometimes you might have to check your speed. You don't want to get up there too quickly because you'll be hitting the ball too low off of the ground.

BLOCKING FIRST SERVE RETURNS

When your opponent is hitting first serves, don't swing at the return of serve. You just block it. Use a short backswing and a short hit and follow through. You're just blocking the ball, because you don't have enough time. When your opponent hits a second serve, he's hitting it a little bit more easily; therefore, you move in on the baseline or a little bit inside the baseline. Since the ball is hit a little more easily, you can swing at it a little harder. Try to get a little more power, and to hit the ball shoulder high as you did on the first serve.

FOREHAND

Never slice your forehand return of serve. Always hit it flat or with a little bit of top spin. Only in a very rare instance, when you're in a lot of trouble and reaching way out to your right, should you possibly slice the forehand return of serve. But never think of it that way. Think of hitting it flat or using top spin.

BACKHAND

On your backhand return of serve, you should be able to slice and drive the ball. Be able to do both well. One of the players that I used to think had a great slice was Pancho Gonzales. His theory was that you should slice low to your opponent's feet. He kept the ball in play and made his opponent hit volleys. A sliced return of serve is usually a very safe shot. He didn't try to hit the ball hard, but he would try to keep it low to his opponents' feet. Ken Rosewall sliced, but he hit the ball a little bit harder. He had kind of a whip slice. He could get it at his opponent's feet like a regular slice, or he could hit it past him. His shot was a little more offensive than Gonzales's. Driving the ball is what you should think of, like Jimmy Connors, who hurts his opponents. Try to get the ball back to the server quickly before he's set. Driving it or top spinning it—either is very effective as an offensive return, and when you're playing well, this is what you should be doing. If you are not hitting the slice well some days, then you should be able to drive and visa versa; therefore, you should be able to do both. If the second serve has a big spin, you should probably slice the ball because it's a little easier to slice if you're unsure of yourself.

HIT AS APPROACH SHOT

The return of serve is hit very much as an approach shot—using the same footwork, and hitting the ball at the same height. After you hit the ball, go through it before you recover.

WHERE TO HIT RETURNS

When you are starting a match, do not try to hit winners—you're nervous and your opponent is nervous; just keep the ball in play. Make your opponent hit a few volleys before he loosens up. Also don't try to hit for the lines at the start of the match. Hit more down the middle because if you hit badly, which you'll do a lot (the ball is coming so fast), the ball will slide off and probably will go way out. So aim down the middle at your opponent's feet. As the match progresses, you gain more confidence; and as you get less nervous, then start hitting for winners a little bit more.

BE READY FOR NEXT SHOT

If you hit a good return of serve, you have to go through that ball, recover, and then get back for the next passing shot. Get back in position quickly. I notice a lot of young players hit a good return of serve, hoping that their opponent will not make a volley; therefore, they just stand around, not ready to hit the next unexpected passing shot. You must be positive all the time: Hit a good return of serve, and be ready to hit other shots.

LOB RETURN WHEN IN TROUBLE

A type of return of serve you never see very much that should be used more often is the lob. This return forces your opponent, who is rushing the net, to make an overhead shot. And sometimes the overhead is hard to hit while coming in very fast. An opponent may be so used to hitting volleys that he's not ready to hit an overhead.

FOOTWORK

On your forehand, you're up on your toes, inching forward as we talked about before. Then when your opponent hits the serve, step out with your right leg and hit. You will hit off your right leg and push forward off it. As far as the backhand is concerned, you should step out with your outside leg (left leg) and then cross over into your front leg (right leg). Do this on both a slice and a top-spin shot. After the hit, hop forward on the right leg, especially after hitting a high bouncing ball.

SECOND SERVE

Talking about the second serve, I mentioned moving in a little closer, maybe even a little bit inside the baseline, depending on how strong your opponent's serve is. Sometimes you can't move in at all if the second serve is very strong. But most of the time it's a little easier, and you can come inside the baseline. When you move in closer, let your opponent see you move in. You want to add a little pressure to the situation. Even if you do not want to move in, let him see you move in, and then get back before he serves. Usually the second serve is hit more gently than the first so you have to move up to it to get to the ball before it spins up any higher than your shoulder since you lose power on balls higher than that. Also on the second serve it's often a good idea to move over a little to your left and run around your backhand to hit your forehand return of serve. It's better to hit with your forehand even if you have a better backhand because when your opponent is serving and volleying it's very difficult for him to read a forehand return of serve. He can volley the backhand return of serve better.

You must let your opponent see you move to your left as though you're going to run around and hit your forehand. Sometimes he'll compensate by coming back to the other side, risking a double fault or any easy serve. Just add more pressure on him, but do not miss returning the serve. If you start missing returns, you're going to take the pressure off.

HOW TO HIT RETURNS

You try to return the first serve by blocking it and hitting it at your opponent's feet. You don't have much time to do anything else, unless you're playing really well. Every once in a while as a match progresses and the opponent is hitting that first serve at you very hard, you can start getting a little bit more over to the left or right, hitting your forehand to his forehand or backhand. But mainly you want to go out to meet the ball, block it, low down to his feet, getting it back to him quickly before he has time to get set, maybe making him hit a half volley. With the second serve you have more time to swing at the ball a little bit and try to go for a winner more often, either down to the opponent's backhand or over to his forehand. You can hurt your opponent more. Every once in a while on that second serve, I really feel that most people pass up a chance to make an offensive shot. You should attack the ball as you would an approach shot. Come into the net, and try to take it away from your opponent. It'll surprise him and put a lot of pressure on him. So use it as an approach shot. Come to the net yourself on the return of serve.

Forehand

If you can count to four, you can return a serve. As far as Count One is concerned, keep your eyes on the ball. As soon as you see the ball coming off the racket, get your racket up. *You pick your racket up* because you're going to hit the ball when it's shoulder high. Then start moving your feet toward the ball, so you're moving with your racket up. Keep your left hand out there close to your head in that triangle we talked about before. Your head is eye level to the ball in this position. Now on Count Two, step out with your right leg and hit the ball with a stroke more or less parallel to the ground. By hitting the ball at shoulder height you do not have to hit it up and over the net. When you hit it, your racket comes over the ball at the last minute to bring it down to your opponent's feet. Keep your head level all the time. You do *not* lift your head up at any time as you maybe would have to do on a regular ground stroke. During all of this time, you're going out to meet the ball.

Backswing for Forehand Return

Backswing for Backhand Return

52 TENNIS: THE BASSETT SYSTEM

Step for Forehand Return

Hit for Forehand Return

Step for Backhand Return

Hit for Backhand Return

The hit is not under the ball; it's right through the ball in the middle part. On Count Three, after you hit the ball, step forward with your left leg. This is different from the regular ground stroke, where you got into your left leg before you hit the ball. Whenever you have to move out to your right quickly and very fast, you should hit off the right leg. When you have enough time, then you hit off your front (left) leg. Count Four, the follow through, is absolutely essential. You lock your follow through up against your shoulder as you did on the regular ground stroke. Do not follow through very far, especially on the first serve because you just want to block it. On the second serve, though, you can follow through a little farther. Continue through the ball after you hit it, and then recover back in the court.

Backhand

Count One, pick your racket up and start moving to the ball. Your racket is up in the same position for both the slice and the drive since you're going to be hitting the ball shoulder high. Your opponent will not know what you're going to hit, either the slice or the drive. Your head is forward, your body is forward, just as we talked about in the discussion of the forehand. And you're moving to the ball. You're still facing the net a little bit. On Count Two when you step into your front (right) leg, your body is turned a little bit more. This is just about when you're ready to hit. You step just a second before you hit the ball. So you're in your right leg on both the slice and the drive before you hit. Your eyes are level to the ball. On Count Three, the hit, you hit the ball off of your front leg. The ball's out in front of you. It's in front of your body, not to the side of it or in back of it, it's out in front of it—maybe out a foot in front of your front

Follow Through for Forehand Return

Follow Through for Backhand Return

leg. You are hitting the ball with a parallel stroke to the ground if you're hitting a drive. If you're hitting a slice, the racket is coming down a little bit. On Count Four, your *follow through*, hit the ball on the drive by coming over the ball just a little with your racket head to knock it down to your opponent's feet. Or, if you slice, the bottom edge should lead a little to get the proper amount of spin. But don't let your bottom edge lead too much, or you'll have too much spin and not enough power. Be sure to complete a strong follow through. If you're returning a first serve, you should not follow through too far. On a second serve, however, you follow through a little farther to get a little more power. Continue on through the shot and then recover back into court—all part of your follow through.

PRACTICE CORRECTLY

Very few people practice the return enough. They'll probably not even hit any returns when warming up. What you should do, since it is such an important shot, is have a friend serve to you, preferably into the court a little. When I'm serving to the players on my team, I'll get a basket of balls, and I'll move inside the baseline about three feet to simulate a hard serve. If I try to serve back at the baseline, then I'll miss a lot of serves. I'll serve to the forehand court to their forehand if that's a problem, and then I'll go to their backhand and will hit to their backhand until they're feeling good about that. Then we'll move over to the backhand court, and we'll do the same thing there—forehands and backhands.

You should practice your return until you have it down, until you're completely confident. Don't skip by it because this shot is too important to forget about. Also, scouting your opponent's serve should be done more often because every opponent winds up differently and serves differently—flat or top spin or slice. So you should see what your opponent is doing, where he's placing the ball on the serve. And then when you get into the match, when you and he are warming up, you try to return a few of his warmup serves just to get ready for that first point, because once that first point starts you can't miss any returns. You can't be surprised by his serve at that time. Every one counts then.

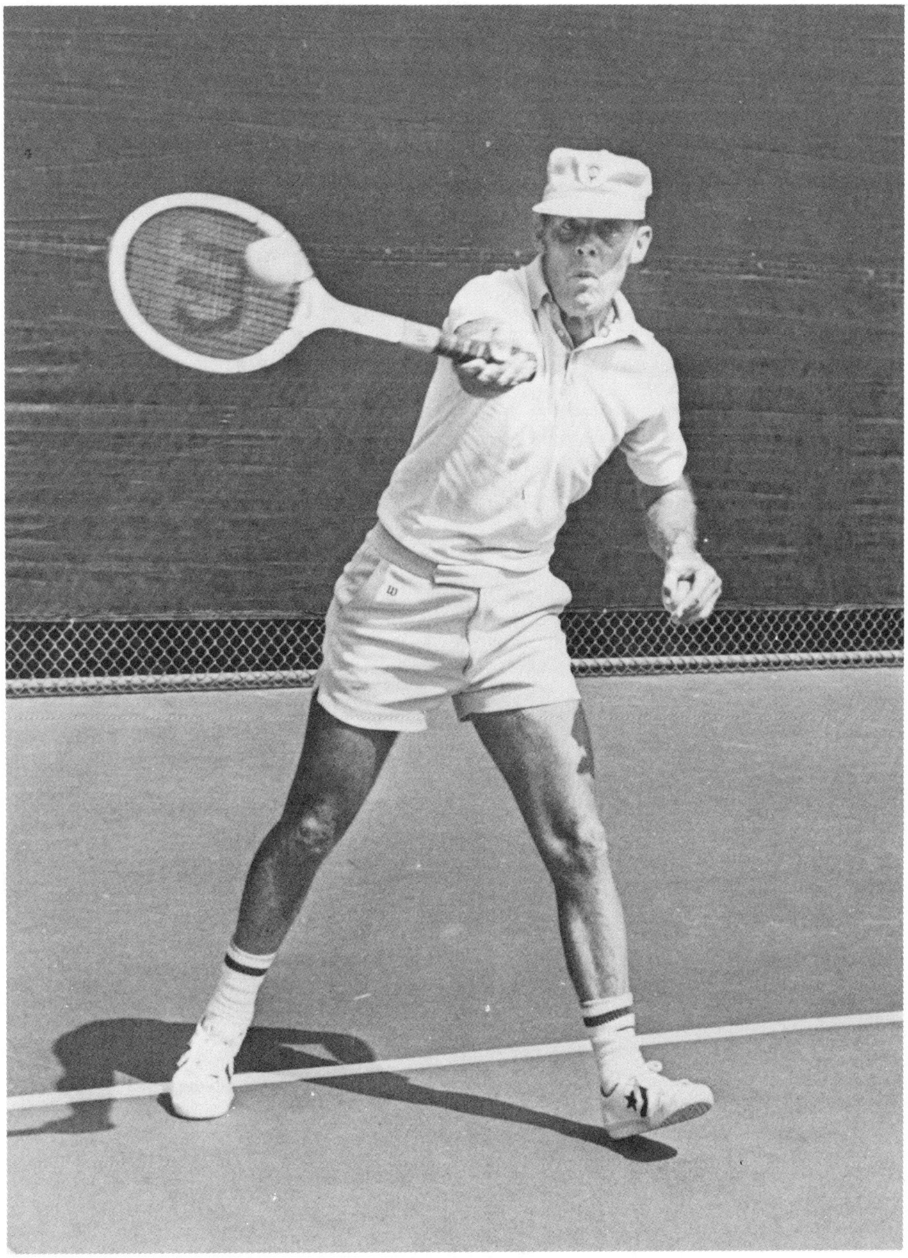

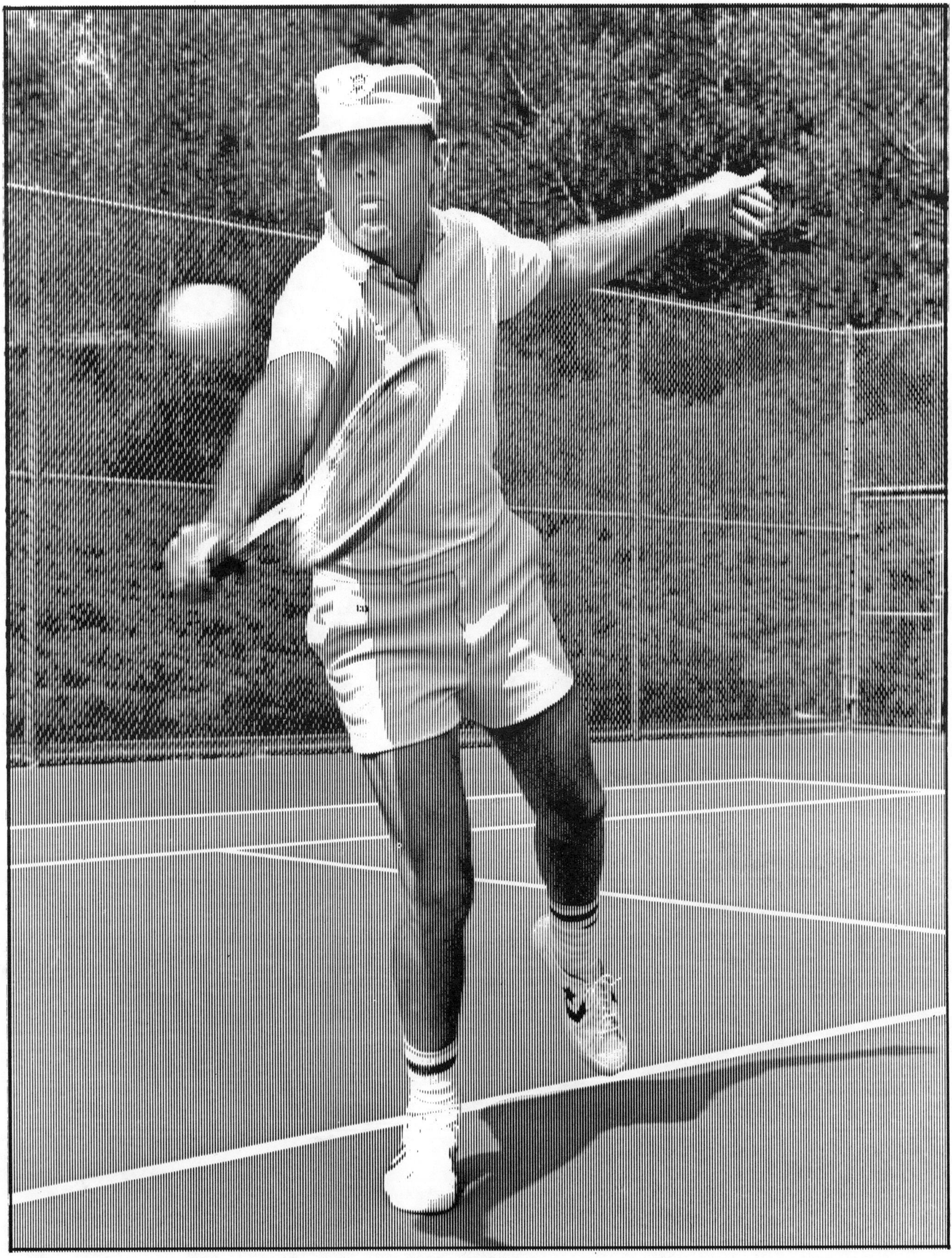

3. Net Play

VOLLEY

A good volley (return of a ball before it bounces) can offset a weak ground stroke and give you an overall winning game. Even the best players aren't strong in every stroke. One of my team players, Bobby Kreiss, had a comparatively weak forehand ground stroke but a powerful forehand volley that more than made up for it. The highly ranked player Billy Martin had a strong two-handed backhand when I coached him, but his one-handed backhand volley was weak. On the other hand, Jimmy Connors has always had stronger backhand ground strokes and backhand volleys than those strokes on his forehand side. After years of coaching all types of players, I've come to the conclusion that a strong ground stroke on either side doesn't necessarily mean a strong volley on the same side. Most players seem to have a weak volley on one side but not necessarily the side with the weak ground stroke. The idea of the volley is the same for both forehand and backhand but this "punch" type shot is played quite differently on the two sides.

Getting ready for the volley is different than getting ready for any other stroke. There are four major differences:

1. The racket must be held further in front of you with your hands chest high and the racket head even with your own head.
2. You should be facing the net with your head out in front of your shoulders and your shoulders out in front of your feet. Eyes should be on a level with the ball, watching it intently from the moment if leaves your opponent's racket.
3. Your knees should be flexed, body weight balanced on the balls of your feet, feet shoulder width apart.
4. Your feet should keep shifting, stepping, shuffling, and moving

constantly so you can get a jump on the ball.

Your best all-around positioning for the volley seems to be inside the service court, two-thirds of the way back from the net. If you're a slower type player, move back closer to the service line. If you're fast and agile, you can move up to a point as close as one-third of the distance from the net. Tall players can position themselves closer to the net than shorter players. Also, pick a position based on your opponent's game. If you're playing a good lobber, play back further from the net.

The grip for the forehand volley can be the regular eastern forehand or the continental. The eastern is best for beginners and intermediates because you don't need the time to change grips. Higher level players should use the continental because it offers more control, feel, and back spin on the ball. Because it's halfway between the forehand and backhand grips, the continental also allows you to move your hand either way very rapidly. Okay, now that you're in the right location and position with the racket in the right grip, let's volley. Even though this shot is short and fast, you need the one-two-three-four count to make it work.

THE BASSETT SYSTEM FOR THE FOREHAND VOLLEY

Count One: Backswing

The instant that the ball leaves your opponent's racket move your hands up from your chest so your right hand is even with your head and your racket head is higher than it. Angle the racket about forty-five degrees off to the right and the racket should be in front of you. Move your left hand up when the right one goes up, and point to the oncoming tennis ball. Keep your hands parallel, palms facing each other and quite close together. Your

Backswing for Forehand Volley

Step for Forehand Volley

hands and your head should form a triangle in front of your face. Remember, the backswing here is very short—about a foot—because the hand moves upward only a few inches and the racket moves back just a few degrees.

Count Two: Step

Just after you raise your racket, step forward to meet the ball. If your feet have been moving and you have time, step toward the net onto your right leg, and then cross over onto your left. If you're rushed, skip the right leg step, and move into your left immediately. Always move forward toward the ball, shifting your weight to that left foot. Sometimes you can run to the ball and then step onto that left foot. Other times, if you're fast enough, you can step out on the right foot, then cross over into the left. Sometimes, however, the ball will be hit so hard you'll only have time for the left step. Be careful not to let the racket move back behind your head as you move forward. Hold that tight triangle with head and hands close together and your head down on a steady line, leaning out over your body. It's important that you go after the ball and not let it come to you. Go get it!! It will give you a psychological lift and will also keep the ball from dropping low. Try to hit the ball when it's still high or rising.

Count Three: Hit

With your racket head above the ball and the racket hand about even with it, punch down and out. Don't stroke, swing, or even move your hand much more than a foot. Just jab it forward to bring the racket *down* on the ball. Your arm and shoulder do very little work, the action stems mostly from your forearm. From backswing to ball contact your hand shouldn't move more than a foot. To make sure you get back spin on the ball hit it with the top edge of the racket

Hit for Forehand Volley

Follow Through for Forehand Volley

slanted back a bit from the bottom edge and to make sure you connect with the ball keep your head low and your eyes level.

Count Four: Follow Through

The racket head should be above your wrist when you hit the ball and about even with it when you've completed the short (about a foot) follow through. Keep your hand relaxed so you can feel the back spin. Then lock your hand so the racket won't twist. At that point your arm should be absolutely straight, but your wrist is laid back a little. The racket head is slanted just back a bit, strings toward the sky. The right amount of back spin will cause the ball to die and fade off when it contacts the ground. However, too much bevel will give the ball too much back spin, and it will pop up when it hits the ground. Make sure you take the racket "through" the ball for six inches to a foot. Don't quit too soon. The step forward and your natural momentum will carry you close to the net as you finish the follow through. Get back to your original position fast so your opponent can't find you in a vulnerable position for a lob.

The volley, like the serve, has a different one-two-three-four rhythm than other strokes. For the volley, get your hands up and your racket moving on the one count. Then, counts two-three-four are ticked off in a fast, continuous motion. The timing should be: one . . . then, two, three, four! If you pause anywhere in the last three counts your volley won't work.

FOOTWORK

Because you don't have much time for your volley return, your footwork is doubly important. The secret lies in little quick steps that keep you on balance but get you to the ball fast. Keep your feet moving at all times when you're in the volley ready position. When you see the ball coming to your forehand side, step out with your right leg first, slide toward the ball with those little quick steps, stop on your right leg, and then step across with the left leg as you hit. If you're short of time or the ball is aimed directly at you, just step onto that left leg in a kind of smooth lunge to give yourself maximum control and time.

FOREHAND VOLLEY STRATEGY

Picking up the *low* forehand volley is a science in itself. You need more back spin to get that ball to pop up off your racket, clear the net, and come down deep in the other court. To do this, you have to bend your knees, get your eyes down level to the ball, and keep them there through the entire stroke. Return of these low volleys is done with more racket touch and less power. Try to place the ball deep into the opposite court so it can't be put away while you're recovering to get into position. Putting it deeply into your opponent's backhand side is best. Remember this is a punch shot. Over-hitting it can too easily put the ball out of the court.

On *high* volleys remember to punch the ball; you don't need as much back spin as on low volleys because the ball is above the net. Every volley needs some back spin unless you're an accomplished player who has mastered the flat volley. From my experience only the pros have reached that plateau of performance and can drive a flat volley without making a costly error. Don't hesitate. If you're not sure whether the ball is going out or not, hit it. If you have the time, go crosscourt with your return because the back spin will force your ball to die when it hits the ground. But if you're in trouble and rushed, go to the deep backhand side and make your opponent scramble for it.

When you're moving into the net after your serve and approach shot, put your first volley back deep, back behind the service line. It's tough to make this first volley a winner because you're running. You have a much better chance of making a point if you put this first volley deep to your opponent's weakest ground stroke (or to his backhand if his ground strokes are equal). For those times when your opponent is way out of court, go to the open part. Otherwise, use your first volley as a setup return so you can get into the net and put away the second or third volley. Watch the pros. They know that trying to put away every volley can lead to bad mistakes.

THE BASSETT SYSTEM FOR THE BACKHAND VOLLEY

The *backhand* volley ready position is much like the forehand. Remember to face the net, head out over the shoulders, shoulders leaning out over your feet. Stay up on the balls of your feet, and keep them moving. If you're a right hander, cradle the racket with your left hand, keeping the left fingertips a few inches above your right hand.

When you see the ball coming to your backhand volley, change your eastern forehand or continental grip to an eastern backhand by lifting the right-hand little finger knuckle up toward you, letting your left hand twist the racket, and then grasping it again with the right hand. The left hand stays on the handle. A lot of players like the compromise continental grip for volleying (and many of them use it very effectively), but I like the changeover. Using the eastern backhand, I like the thumb to go up the handle at a forty-five degree angle to give the stroke more power.

Count One: Backswing

Most of the backhand backswing is identical to the forehand, except you're going to the other side. As with the forehand, face the net and keep your feet moving. Move your hands up in front of your face even with the oncoming ball as soon as it leaves your opponent's racket, as you also did with the forehand. The racket head should be above your head about forty-five degrees to the left and a little behind the hand. At no time in the *volley backhand* do your hands or arms go behind your body. Instead, they stay out in front of your face.

Backswing for Backhand Volley

Count Two: Step

Just before hitting the ball, shift weight to your right leg, step toward the oncoming ball and the net, and turn your body a little sideways. Be careful not to step parallel to the net, but do move forward. If there's time, step out first with your left leg, and then cross over it with your right. If you're hurried, just step forward, and cross over with the right leg, skipping the left leg preliminary. Ideally, the perfect timing would allow you to move your feet

Step for Backhand Volley

Hit for Backhand Volley

in little quick steps toward the ball, step out with the left leg, and then cross over with the right. Unfortunately, the speed of today's game seldom gives you the leisure for all of that, but whenever you can go through that entire series, do it. The result is much better position, balance, control, and approach to the ball. When you turn slightly sideways there will be a tendency to lay your arms and hands behind your body. Fight that urge. Keep them out in front of your body. As with the forehand, don't wait for the ball to come to you but go get it before it peaks over the net and you're stuck with a low volley to return. Catch the ball high, and step into it positively, up on your toes and stepping across with your right foot. Remember to get your eyes level with the ball, and keep them there.

Count Three: Hit

When you start forward with the racket head to make contact with the ball, release your left hand and straighten your right arm a little, turning your racket hand so the back of it faces away from you, toward the net. Bring the racket head out and down on the ball with the bottom edge leading the top to get a slice. Watch this bottom edge lead because too much of it will "over-slice," and a popped up ball won't die when it hits the ground. At the moment of contact, the racket head should be still above the wrist but on its way down to a position even with it. Your body should be leaning out over your right leg, all of your weight on it. The left leg carries no weight at all. Move your head toward the ball, and hold your eyes unblinkingly on it all the way through the hit.

Count Four: Follow Through

For the entire backhand volley, your racket head moves only a couple of feet, and the follow through part takes up six

NET PLAY 63

Follow Through for Backhand Volley

inches to a foot of that but *no more!* At the completion of your follow through, the racket head should be even with your wrist, and the bottom edge of the racket should be leading the top edge. For low volleys the bottom edge will lead a little more than for high ones because you need more back spin to salvage the shot. Your arm should be completely straight by now, but the racket ends up laid back a little at an angle from the arm. Make sure you get the back spin feel and go through the ball before recovering to get back into position. Don't ruin a good backhand volley by trying to recover too soon or by lifting your head and pulling up before you've finished the follow through.

The backhand volley has the same one (pause) two, three, four rhythm as the forehand volley. It's backswing—then step, hit, follow through. The last three counts come together in one fast routine. Practice the backhand volley motion even when you don't have a racket or a court. Do this by putting both hands in front of your face, and then pulling back on your right hand with the left. When tightly pulled, snap the right hand out just as if you were hitting a ball. It's somewhat like pulling the string of a bow. The left hand pulls the string back, and the right hand acts like the arrow, straightening out forward and downward very fast.

FOOTWORK

The footwork for the backhand volley is very similar to the forehand volley, but reversed. It's important that you start moving on your toes, stay on your toes, and then cross over. Wherever possible on the backhand volley, take those little quick steps toward the ball; step out with your left leg; then cross the right one over it and toward the net. With less time just step out with the left and cross over with the right. If you have no time, just cross over with the right. Obviously, the more positioning you can do the more control you'll have over your backhand volley return. Your feet will react to your eyes. If your eyes pick up your opponent's ball too late, your feet can't make up the tardiness. See the ball coming, and get your feet moving fast.

STRATEGY

Through the years I've learned that there is a definite inner psychology to hitting a successful volley. Attacking the ball gives a player a positive response while waiting for it seems to create a negative reaction, almost a fear of the ball. The key to a successful volley seems to be interception rather than reaction. *Get that ball before it gets you* seems to be a motto that could work here.

When intercepting, try to hit the ball a bit harder than it was hit to you. This seems to reinforce that positive feeling. Don't, however, try to kill it or make every volley a putaway winner. This leads to expensive misses and mistakes. Low volleys are difficult to hit hard but try laying into those high ones for a feeling of self confidence and game control.

Finally, practice your volley strokes as much as you do the ground strokes. A good volley can give you a balanced back-and-up game and is worth equal time.

Forehand, or backhand, don't try to put away that first volley when you're running into the net. It's too difficult a shot. Just keep the ball in play, and then when you get to the net ready position, punch hard or try placement of the volley for points. That opportunity might come on the second volley or the third or even the tenth, but don't try that "sure" point until you're in a position to control your shot.

Remember the differences between the forehand and backhand volleys. On the forehand you do not hold the racket with both hands, but those hands are both up in front of your face, palms facing each other forming a triangle with your head. On the backhand volley both hands are holding onto the racket with your head tucked into that triangle of left hand, right hand, and the head is easier to form since both hands are holding onto the racket. On the forehand, many players seem to have trouble stepping across onto their left leg. When they get mixed up or in trouble they settle for stepping out and hitting off of the right leg. This can throw off the timing and control of the entire stroke. If you find this a problem, work on it. Crossing over with the left leg is not that difficult and the results for your forehand volley will be well worth it.

HALF VOLLEY

I think most coaches will agree that this is the toughest shot in tennis. Your timing must be perfect. Although the half volley is played low—picked up within a foot of the ground—it is not played totally like a low volley. Technically, a volley is hit *before* and the half volley *after* the ball bounces. To get off a successful half volley you must hit the ball just after it leaves the ground. Generally, you're up at the net, and your opponent slams one very fast right at your feet. You have split seconds to get to it, under it, lift it high enough to clear the net so it comes back down in the court and is still placed so it's not a putaway for the other guy. Now, that's what I mean by perfect timing.

The ready position is the same as the volley ready; up at the net ready to hit a volley return. Let's say your opponent manages to lay in a short, low, fast one, and you're caught. You can't move up fast enough to play it as a ground stroke. The only answer is the half volley. Although it's the most difficult shot to master, if you don't learn it, opponents can wreck you. But, if you do have a good half volley you can demoralize *them*.

THE BASSETT SYSTEM FOR FOREHAND AND BACKHAND HALF VOLLEY

Count One: Backswing

Make sure you play the ball when it is in front of you. Don't let it get in back. There is no windup on this backswing. Instead, you take the racket straight back a short distance, roughly half the distance of a ground stroke backswing. On the forehand try to make that little triangle with your hands and head. On the backhand hold on to the racket with both hands. Don't raise the racket head above your wrist, but instead, drop it below that wrist as it goes back. Bend your knees, and get down very low with body weight forward and balanced and head down to get a good look at the ball. If you must "close" to the ball, use those small, quick steps we've talked about so you don't overrun it or get yourself off balance.

Backswing for Forehand Half Volley

Backswing for Backhand Half Volley

Count Two: Step

On the forehand side try to step into your left leg before hitting the ball. If you've had to break wide to the right and are running you won't be able to do this. Hit off the right leg, instead. Make sure your racket doesn't go back any farther when you take that step. On the backhand side, step forward into your right leg either while running or if you're in a set position. Make sure again that your weight shifts onto that forward leg.

Count Three: Hit

Get your racket head down under the ball then lift it with a short stroking action, putting enough top spin on the ball to get it over the net. Stay away from back spin here. Make sure your head and body stay down through the hit. If you look up, you're going to lift up and destroy the shot.

Count Four: Follow Through

Keep your racket on the ball for six inches to a foot after you contact it. End with a short follow through, which goes only far enough to point where you're hitting. When finished, your racket should be higher than the contact point and the top edge should be tilted forward slightly to help put top spin on the ball. Make sure you have a strong follow through. A blocking-only action won't work.

PRACTICE

Although there is a general chapter on practice techniques later in this book, I wanted to make a few comments about practicing the half volley because the shot is so difucult. Alan Fox, a former intercollegiate champion from UCLA practiced this stroke better than any player I've ever seen. In practice, he would position himself behind the service line to play his volleys and also hit half volleys as the returns came close to his feet. Try it. Get a

Step-Hit for Forehand Half Volley

Follow Through for Forehand Half Volley

Step-Hit for Backhand Half Volley

Follow Through for Backhand Half Volley

few feet behind the service line to volley, and you'll find a great many returns must be played as half volleys because they'll come in short and low.

I've had a lot of players who couldn't hit this shot very well and a few who could stroke it superbly. One of the best half volleyers I ever coached (and USC coach George Toley agreed) was a Northern Californian named Gary Rose. He not only could hit the shot, but he often put his half volleys away for winners. And this wasn't against shabby players. He half volleyed points away from court giants like Bob Lutz and Stan Smith. He made it look easy. Jeff Austin was another fine volleyer who couldn't always convert the shot into a point but who hardly ever missed it, always controlled the return, and placed it back deep to his opponent. His secret was a good short backswing and a solid follow through. He remembered to play the ball while it was in front of him and to stay down low.

Paradoxically enough, most good volleyers don't play the stroke very often. They're also good enough tennis players so they don't get trapped. They're either up to hit a volley or back to hit the ground stroke, especially in singles. For doubles, though, the half volley is needed often, and if you're going to be a good doubles partner, it's a stroke you must practice, learn, and own.

OVERHEAD SMASH

The *ready position* is exactly the same as the volley ready position and the *grip* is your choice of eastern forehand or the continental. As you know from earlier chapters, I prefer the eastern forehand for most forehand shots.

Count One: Backswing

When you see that lob coming, turn sideways, and get your feet moving toward the ball. Don't wind up as though you're going to serve, but instead, run with both hands in the air about head high. Your left hand should be aimed at the ball, and the right hand should be holding the racket up and ready for the hit. Turn your side, arms up, and move to the ball quickly.

Count Two: Step

After using quick steps to get into position with the ball in front and a little to the right of you, plant your right foot and push off and step into your left foot. Keep your head up and eyes on the ball as you step forward. Keep your left arm pointing at the ball, telling the racket head where to go. Be careful not to pull your head or left arm down too soon because you don't want to quit on this shot too soon.

Count Three: Hit

The hitting action starts the way it does in the serve; by moving your right elbow up and forward. This cocks your wrist and also puts the racket down behind your back to get the whip action needed for this shot. Like so many other strokes, don't wait for the ball to come to you. In this case, stretch and go *up* to get it. Keeping your head up and eye on the ball, swing the racket head flat through the ball. Occasionally, you can slice it crosscourt, but most of the time hit this shot flat.

Count Four: Follow Through

Stay with the ball after you hit it and control the direction of the ball by snapping your wrist and the racket head in the same direction. Finish the follow through with the racket head coming down and across your left leg, like a service ending. After your hit, swing the right leg forward and ahead of your left leg, and shift your weight there. It sounds tricky but it isn't. It's just a jump with the legs and body weight reversing. Practice it a few times,

68 TENNIS: THE BASSETT SYSTEM

Backswing for Overhead Smash

Step for Overhead Smash

Hit for Overhead Smash

Follow Through for Overhead Smash

and you'll find it comes easily and naturally.

FOOTWORK

Remember how you run forward and sideways at the same time to get to your forehand or to a volley? For the overhead smash, you run backwards and sideways because the lob is generally aimed over your head. Get moving with those small, quick steps when the ball comes off your opponent's racket, and keep moving until you reach the ball. Don't *reach* for the ball, and don't let it get behind you. Keep moving until you're behind it.

Quite often you won't have time to get set, and that's when you use the *scissors kick* for this return. When the opponent lobs the ball in back of you very fast get your arms up, turn sideways, and jump up, pushing off your right leg, then hit. Repeat: arms up, turn sideways, jump up off your right foot, hit. Landing on your left leg with your right leg up and in front of you will maintain your balance. Many top ranked players like the scissors kick because the jump and hit are combined in one reflex action. It also gives them good psychological momentum because they're going up to meet the ball instead of waiting for it to come down. The scissors kick overhead smash is the only effective answer to the fast lob return. Practice and learn it. Chances are good you'll use it often and save points you used to lose.

STRATEGY

As I mentioned, the overhead is a physically tiring shot, especially when you practice it over and over. But, because of its importance you should get good at it. If your opponent notices that you have a weak or nonworking overhead, you can expect a great many lobs and a great many lost points. The more this happens, the more confident he's going to become, and the more discouraged you'll get. Even if you've put your opponent in trouble and he's throwing up lobs as desperate answers, he'll switch to using them offensively if you can't return them.

Practice hitting the overhead mostly to the traditionally weak backhand side. However, don't concentrate totally there. If you develop a habit of hitting to one side, your opponent will soon pick that up and adjust to handle it. Mix in slices and flat drives to the forehand court, as well. Sometimes when you're in trouble, hitting the overhead smash deeply right down the middle will keep your opponent from getting a good angle on his next shot and you can keep your net position. This is especially good if you're not going to get away a good smash. Trying to put the overhead away every time you get one can be a mistake. If you're not in total control, you may be handing a free point to your opponent.

The only times you should let the ball bounce are when it comes to you short and straight down or when it's so deep that you need time to get back behind it. All other times, hit it in the air. Because the stroke is a bit different, *practice* hitting those "bounce" overheads the same amount of time you practice hitting them in the air.

Finally, to develop a strong overhead, get in good physical shape. A fine young player named Billy Martin developed both strength and skill at the overhead by hitting it hours at a time as his father lobbed balls at him. Jimmy Connors developed his now effective overhead through determined practice and through physical conditioning. There are many ways to get into better physical shape. I've included information on conditioning later in the book, and you might read it for tips on what the best young amateurs do to increase their strength and endurance.

Although the overhead smash and the

serve have a lot of motion in common, the same player might not always master both. Billy Martin's serve is comparatively weak, but as I said above, his overhead is, excuse me, uh, smashing. Arthur Ashe has both an excellent serve and an excellent overhead. One of my great players, Jeff Borowiak, was so sure of his overhead he'd hardly look at it—while I painfully looked away, expecting him to miss it. He seldom, if ever, did. Peter Fleming, who recently won the NCAA Doubles Championship for UCLA, handles in-the-air overheads extremely well but has trouble with that shot if the ball bounces. Others on my teams hit the ball strongly on the bounce but not while it's in the air. Since even the best players have trouble with some form of the overhead, you can see why it's important for you to practice it both ways.

BACKHAND OVERHEAD

Up until now we've been talking about the forehand overhead; the one you'll use the most. Every once in a while you'll be forced into a backhand overhead. Try to stay away from it even if you have to run around the ball to play it on your forehand side. The backhand overhead has little power and is definitely not a putaway shot. I remember when Bobby Riggs was going to play Margaret Court in that highly publicized "Battle of the Sexes," that big, strong Australian girl practiced high backhand returns and the backhand overhead for hours because she and her coach, Dennis VanderMeer, believed Riggs might put a great number of balls to that traditionally weak stroke.

Don't try to put the backhand overhead away or even make a good shot of it. Getting it back deep and keeping your regular net position is more than enough to ask. One tip: Keep your feet moving and lean forward when you hit the backhand overhead. Watch Jimmy Connors when he hits this stroke. He's excellent at it.

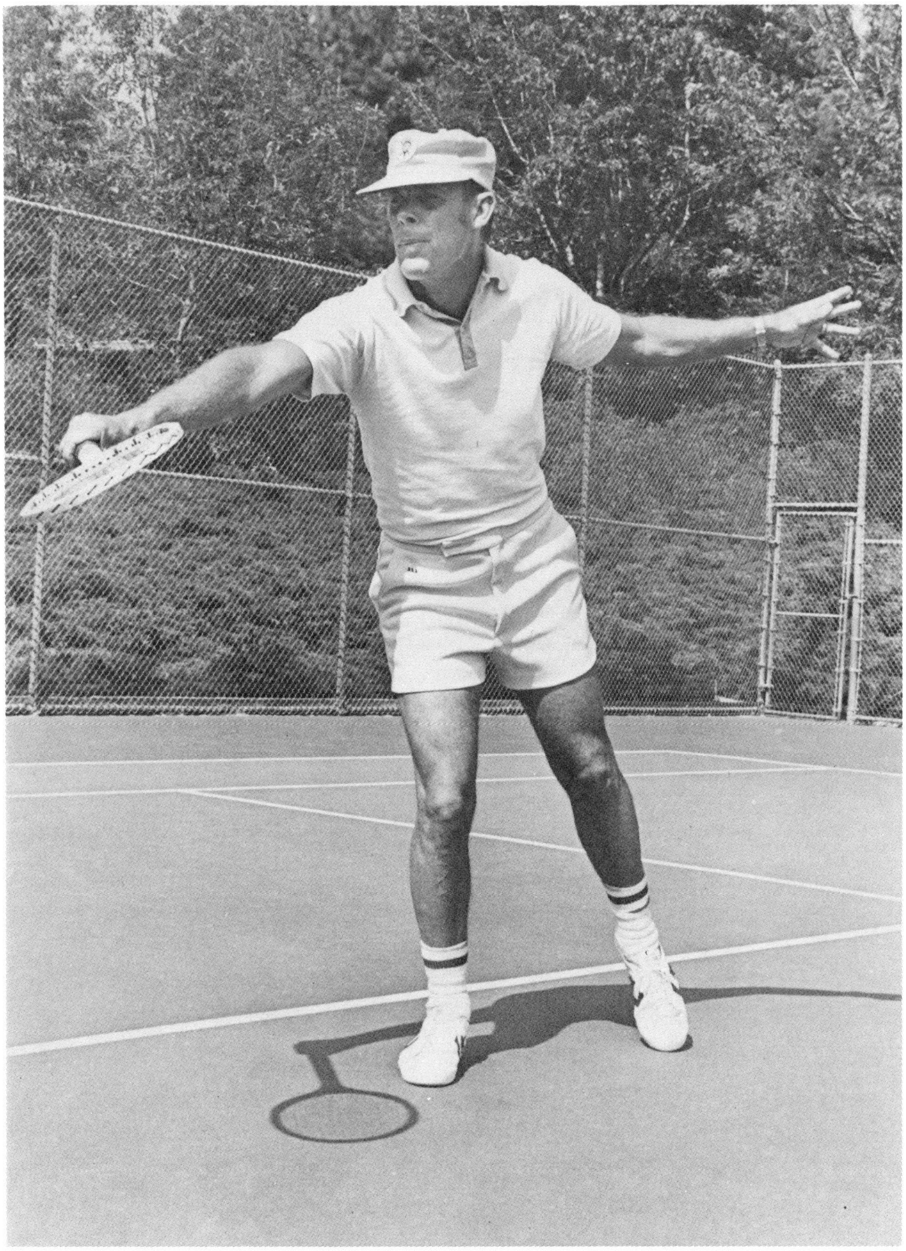

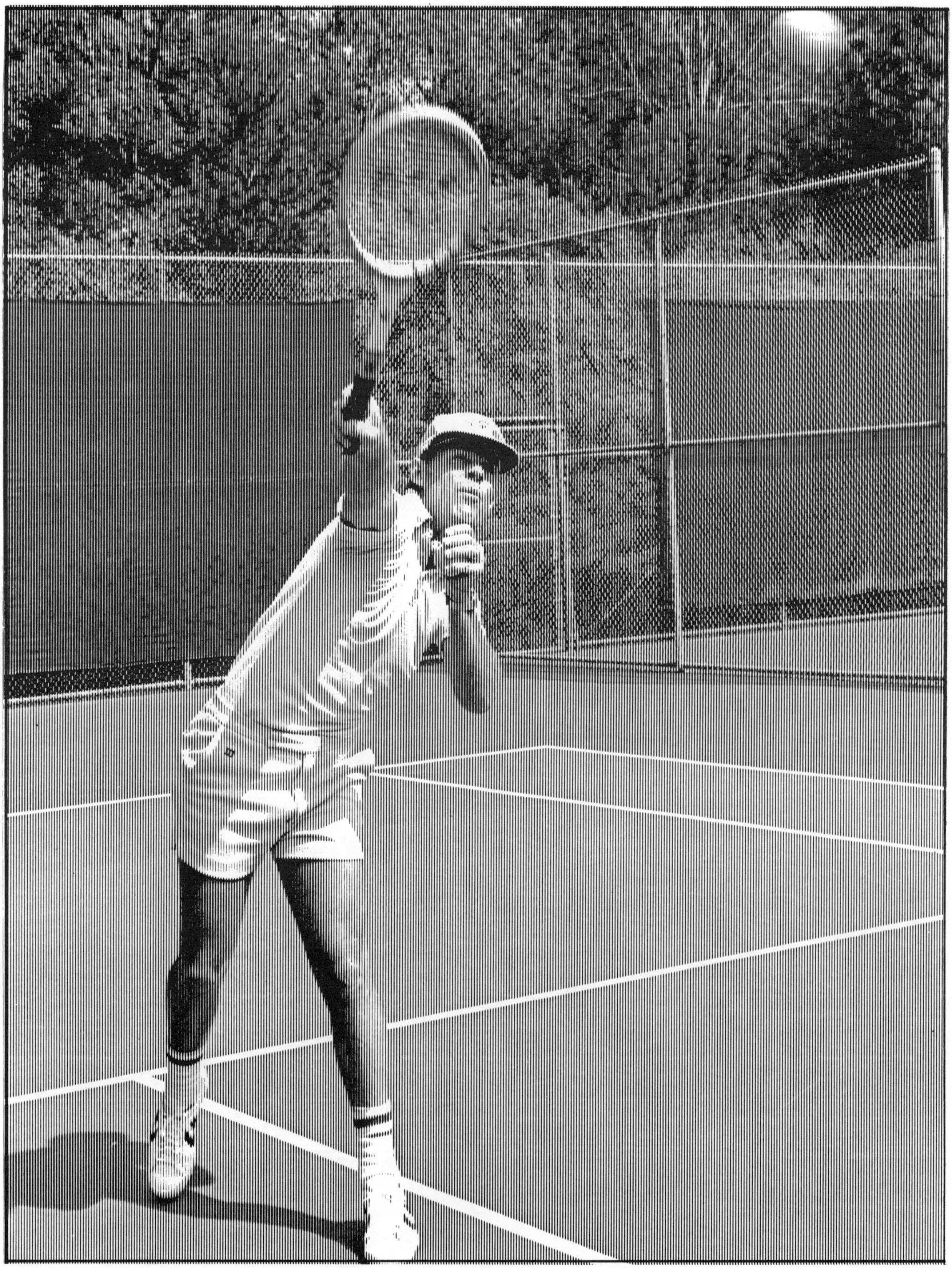

4. Position and Footwork

Coaching members of one of the nation's top college tennis teams is rewarding, but it is not easy. College tennis has become an increasingly complicated game played by highly developed, truly skilled athletes. The differences between the best person on the squad and the weakest are not that great. They generally differ in nuances, subtleties, and inches rather than grand variances. A slight change of swing here, a good attitude there, a minor adjustment of racket or timing can change a player's game—and his ranking—completely. I've seen it happen too many times. It's my job to find those small errors and to suggest changes to the players. Yet even the best college players get set in their ways or take a long time to learn new habits. Two of the most troublesome areas lie in court position and in footwork. Some of the greatest improvements seem to happen here. Because these two areas seem to be of such importance to the overall game, I have added this special chapter, which concentrates on these critical areas.

POSITION

Some coaches, especially at the popular new tennis camps and schools, draw chalked X's on the courts and tell the students to stand exactly there for certain strokes and over here for others. I wish it were that simple. The longer I've been around tennis the more I've learned that correct position depends upon the individual player's speed, height, service, net game, strength, strokes, athletic ability, and brain. It also depends upon his opponent's control of the same things. Many good college team players are agile enough to get totally out of position on a shot and still get back into the court for a return. Tall team players do better when they play close to the net. Players with a powerful serve can come into the net right away and very often. Poor servers can't get there as easily. A player who can volley should be up, playing a net game and the person who doesn't shouldn't. That's called *positioning your strengths,* but it doesn't always work. For example, players with excellent forehands and weak backhands should not always run around that backhand to use their strongest stroke because it gets them out of position. So, point one, the *way* you play goes quite a distance in determining *where* you play.

Point two, the way *your opponent* plays also determines where you should play. If you're up against a player with good ground strokes, then it's to your advantage to get him up to the net, using his weaker shots. To do this, try drop shots until you've moved him into that disadvantageous spot. Should that opponent have weak ground strokes, then keep him in the back court by all means. Move them around by angling the ball to different sides and come up to the net yourself to put away those easy ground strokes he's sending back. Obviously, if your opponent has a strong serve you move back away from the baseline. A weak serve demands that you move up, even into the court. So you see, the way your opponent plays does also affect your position.

Most tennis players have habits or tendencies, and you can position yourself to take advantage of them. If your opponent is very fond of the forehand crosscourt shot, position yourself to the right of center on your court, and you can start adding up your points. If that opponent tends to go down the line on his backhand, adjust over in that direction. Of course, don't overadjust on any of these moves and get yourself completely out of position for the next return. To adjust properly, move over a little rather than overdoing it. For the opponent who just loves to throw up those skyball lobs, play back from the net. If you're up against a real hitter, move back in the court to handle that power, but if you get caught when he starts dropping short ones just over the net, begin playing up.

Try to read what the opponent is going to hit and where. Pros and advanced players can very often prespot the coming shot from the action of their opponent's racket. If he drops the racket head while he's stepping out to meet the ball in front of him, chances are his return will go crosscourt and you can be there, smiling, ready for a slick return. When the ball gets behind your opponent and he's trying to slice it (and you can read it by the racket action), it will either go down the line or up into a lob. Learn to read the angle, speed, and attitude of the racket head to get a jump on the oncoming ball. However, don't depend on this totally. There are too many good—and bad—players who look like they're hitting one stroke but get off another. The dropped racket head, in talented or in novice hands, can also mean a down the line. Getting to know your particular opponent and his responses is the best observation you can make.

Try to keep your court "balanced" as much as possible and take advantage of an unbalanced opponent's court to score points. When you're balanced, you're in position to play a return from either side. A great many points can be lost if you're continually hitting out of position and rushing to get back into the court. It's simple for your opponent to put the ball behind you so you can't turn around in time to get it. When recovering back into the court, don't move too fast and get out of control, but don't move too slowly either, or he'll put it to the open court away from you.

Where your opponent goes after he hits a shot can be important to the way you play it. Advanced players not only watch the ball coming in but also observe where the other player is going. If he's not coming into the net, you can get to the ball and get off a nice steady shot without hurrying. If he is coming in to the net, your shot must be better planned and stroked to get by him. One other advantage of taking a split second to observe the other player is to see if he's in trouble. If he's had a difficult time getting your shot or is out of position or out of control, just hit the ball to the open side where he can't reach it. While doing this, move closer to the net so even if he does get off a weak return you're in position to handle it. In the reverse situation, where he has you in trouble, realize it and get back farther in the court to handle that shot.

Caught out of position, many players just give up and abandon the point to the other guy. This is a waste. One clever answer to this is to fake your body one way and then start running the other just before he hits the ball. If his reflexes aren't fast enough, he'll hit the way you want. A clever variation of this is to fake one way, start the other, stop and stay where you are. Sometimes your opponent will get confused and hit the ball right back to you. However, only do this when you are in real trouble.

RALLIES

One of the major purposes of the rally is to move your opponent around until you can get him out of position. There are some good general rules about rally positioning that can help you stay in court and in command.

Back Court Rallies

Most back court-to-back court rallies are backhand-to-backhand, because crosscourt backhands are easy and safe to hit. Generally, you should be standing anywhere from two to ten feet behind the baseline; the deeper you are, the steadier you can be. If you want to develop more offense or hit deeper shots, move up, even move inside the baseline if your opponent starts to have trouble. However, if you've hit a weak backhand crosscourt, return behind the baseline to give yourself more time and room to run down his return.

In addition to the depth, start your backhand rally standing a little to the left of the center line. Most players—generally including your opponent—have a difficult time hitting backhands down the line to your forehand. Instead, they will tend to go crosscourt to your backhand. Standing to the left of center gives you a better angle on the ball without totally surrendering the forehand court.

When you get off a good backhand shot that forces your opponent to scurry and stretch, then move over to the right of center and inside the baseline a little. If he's in real trouble, move even more inside. That's probably where his weak return will end up, and you'll be waiting for it. On the other hand, if you hit a short, poor backhand crosscourt, your opponent might very well come in and hit a down-the-line approach shot. Be prepared for this and balance the court by moving to your right. Also watch for a drop shot. Opponents love to do this after you've set up a poor return, especially if they're closing in on the net anyway. When you're hitting forehands crosscourt to your opponents forehand, stand nearer the center line. For backhands crosscourt, move to the left a bit. The tendency of most players (including your opponent) is to hit forehands down the line more often than they hit backhands down the line.

Now for depth. If you're just trying to play a steady rally to move your opponent around and finally to wear him down, play those rallies from behind your baseline. But if you're pressing offensively and getting off hard shots, move up to within a foot or two of the baseline. Also, when you do get off an excellent shot that forces your opponent to reach, move inside the baseline and a bit to the side of your shot to pick off his return. Remember, however, when *you* are forced into a weak return, hasten back into the court because your opponent is probably going to smack a deep approach shot. But be careful here. He could also go to an unexpected drop shot and put you in real trouble.

Net—Back Court Rallies

When you serve or hit an approach shot and come into the net while your opponent is still back court, you need position adjustments to handle his returns. If you've hit to his forehand side, move to the left of the center line. Should your shot move him way out of court, then move a yard or so to the left because chances are his return will come down the line on that side. When you've hit the ball to his backhand, move right a little, especially if you've put him in trouble. The closer you play to the net the easier it is for you to control the game but watch out for the lobber. An opponent who can throw up successful lobs is an opponent who can hurt your net game.

In the reverse situation where *your opponent is at the net and you're back court*, play it close to the baseline. When he hits to your backhand, get over and get the ball, then swiftly return to your center position to balance the court. The same holds true when you hit a crosscourt passing shot either with your backhand or forehand. Every time you're forced out of that center baseline position by your opponent's placement or your return, scuttle back there fast and get the court balanced. If you manage a good passing shot and catch your opponent unprepared, move into the court, expecting a weak volley which you can hit away for a winner.

POSITION FUNDAMENTALS

Forehand

For safe, steady forehands, position yourself two to ten feet behind the baseline. For harder hits or a stronger attack, move closer to the baseline or even inside of it.

Backhand

The same as the forehand stroke regardless of whether you're hitting top spins or slices.

Volley

To hit offensive volleys for putaways play up close to the net. In this position be alert for lobs.

Half Volley

Play this shot at the net also, but adjust left or right depending upon your opponent's location. If he's over to his backhand side, move to your right a foot to three feet depending on his exact position. Shift to the left if he's to his forehand side. Play the half volley at or near your service line, when you can. Positioning yourself closer to the net increases your chances of putting the ball into the net.

Overhead

Run into a position so you can hit the ball while it's in front of and to the right of you. Try not to reach for it, but do keep moving forward when you hit. When returning a high overhead that comes down near your baseline, let it bounce first to give yourself a better return and better position for the next shot.

Drop Shot

If you're positioned at the baseline, do not hit the drop shot unless you're trying to bring your opponent up to the net. The best time to hit it is when you're at the service line or even closer to the net.

Approach Shot

Stay away from the approach shot

when you're deep or behind the baseline. It takes too long for you to get to the net. The ideal place to stroke this shot is when you're close to the net; the closer the better. Wait until you get a short return before using your approach shot.

Serve

Changing position occasionally at the baseline can often confuse your opponent and upset his timing. Stand close to your center line and serve down the middle of your opponent's service courts to gain points. Moving out from that center line gives you stronger angles. Remember, an imaginary line drawn across your toes will show you the angle at which your serve will go. If you miss the first serve, play the second one from the spot that's giving you the highest percentage of successful ones.

Service Return

Having trouble with your opponent's serve? Move back to give yourself more time and room to get it. If his serve is slow or uncertain, move in to attack it. Most players have service habits. If he tends to serve wide, play wide. If he hits a lot of center-line shots, play there. If he's serving often to your backhand, adjust and be prepared for it. If you deliberately position yourself very deep or very wide to the right or the left, your opponent will often have trouble with depth perception or perspective. Too, he may sense an opportunity for an ace and try hitting the open court. If he's watching you too much, he can easily hit the serve wrong.

Passing Shot

Move up close to the baseline for passing shots so the ball doesn't peak and drop before you get it. The idea is to move in and hit the ball while it's rising—especially against good players.

Lobs

Position yourself at or just inside the baseline to hit offensive lobs. This gets the ball over your opponent's head before he can recover for an overhead smash. However, for defensive lobs, get far back behind the base line so you can get under the ball, hit it hard, and still have time to recover back into court.

If you hit an offensive lob and you're somewhat out of position, try for a winner because it's difficult to recover rapidly. If you're drastically out of position, then throw up a high lob that will give you time to get back into court balance. Don't try for a putaway in this situation, however, because it seldom works.

FOOTWORK

Earlier chapters have covered some elementary footwork for each stroke, but the many complex ways to cover court and move through shots is so important I believe footwork needs a special subsection of its own.

The single most important rule I can give you is to keep your feet moving all the time, *all* the time. The only tennis player who should be standing around is somebody waiting for a court.

It may be a long distance between your head and your feet, but nothing controls footwork more than your eyes. Your feet can't see the ball coming so your eyes have to tell them. This eye-foot communication is so important that some slow players with good eyes can get to the ball much faster than fast players with lazy eyes. Total visual alertness is absolutely necessary to a good tennis player. Jimmy Connors's visual acuity is so advanced he's moving toward the ball at the split second it leaves his opponent's racket. He's not super fast but he's always where he should be when the ball arrives. Billy Martin is another player whose sharp eyesight controls his feet. I've had other players who were faster than these two, but who couldn't get to the ball as rapidly because their eyes weren't doing their job.

For good footwork, the rest of your body has to be in good shape as well. Physically, if you're in top condition, the constant motion won't exhaust you. Psychologically, if you're in good condition, you're not afraid to stretch, to reach, to extend your limits, to outplay your usual game (and your opponent) by using superior physical strength and stamina to go after and to retrieve even the toughest shots. Getting those "impossible" shots does wonders for your own confidence and erodes your opponent's belief in himself. Players who get to every ball are players with good footwork. Getting every ball puts extreme pressure on the opponent, and eventually he'll start to feel it and miss easy shots.

Too, good footwork opens up opportunity shots. For example, if you hit a backhand and stand around watching its graceful flight, you won't be ready to return your opponent's weak shot. If you'd been moving, your answer to his weak return could easily be a passing shot or an advantageous approach shot. When you're moving, short balls are perfect for putaways; but if you're not moving, they can plop in for points. Getting to the ball earlier and faster gives you the opportunities to make strong offensive shots out of weak defensive ones.

Getting a jump on the ball by using your eyes gives you a chance to glide instead of running hard to retrieve it. When you hit a ball on the run your eyes usually aren't set and you don't get a good look at it. Gliding for the ball keeps your head and eyes from bobbing up and down, keeps your stroke steadier, and even conserves strength.

For ground strokes, there are three basic ways to move to the ball. With all of them, you move with your body facing the net as much as possible and your racket in the beginning of the backswing position. Al-

Slide Skip

Crossover

Sprint

though you may have to partially turn to run after a ball, try keeping your body facing the net. Going to the forehand side, step out first with the outside leg, the right leg. For the backhand side step out first with the left.

One way to get to the ball is a sort of slide skip in which you never cross your feet. You'll see advanced players move this way because they're usually in good position and have little court to cover. In addition to your body, also keep your feet facing the net the entire time you're moving.

The second way to run is used when you have more distance to cover. Here you must cross your legs and cover court until you get to the ball. If you watch advanced players, you'll also see them use this crossover step to get around quickly and still maintain balance.

The third method is used when the ball is hit far from you and sprinting is the only way you're going to get to it. Here, it's almost impossible to continue facing the net because you're forced to turn and run fast toward the ball.

For all three approaches always move with the racket in the backswing position (Count One) described in earlier chapters. Your racket should be back a bit, ready to go into your full backswing as soon as you arrive at the ideal position to hit the ball. Use long fast steps to get close to the ball, then switch to those quick short ones so you can adjust for windage or back spin or even misjudging how and where the ball is going to land.

Footwork doesn't stop after you've hit the ball. Remember the footwork on Count Four (Follow Through)? After you've hit a forehand (off your forward left leg), bring your right leg up even with the left, and then recover your court position. On the backhand remember to hit off your forward right leg; then bring the left one up even with it before recovering. This movement finishes off the follow through and helps you keep going through the ball. Don't wait around to admire your stroke. Get moving. Recover. Get back and balance the court before your opponent can spot a likely putaway.

Even if you've hit a tournament-winning ball, expect it to come back. I think one of the reasons Jimmy Connors is such a winner is that he's disappointed if his opponent doesn't send up a return. Jimmy likes the game of tennis and likes hitting the ball. This is a positive reaction, and it creates positive results. Players who hope they've hit winners or pray that their opponent will make a mistake are thinking negatively, and their game usually goes that way.

One special time to concentrate on your continuous foot motions is when you're in an important match, the outcome isn't certain, and the big point is coming up.

For some reason, at this point, many players get tense and stiff and stop moving. The best way to come out ahead in that match is to move more, not stop.

Consistency in strokes is one of the secrets of a good tennis player and consistency in good footwork is the secret behind that secret. Moving as and when you should helps you get off consistently good strokes. You can hit the same stroke the same way and perfect it. Bad footwork will force you to hit behind you one time, out in front of you another, or handcuff you a third. You can't develop a good ground-stroke game if you can't hit the ball the correct way. Being there and being ready for it is the best way to develop ideal strokes.

Let's review basic footwork for the fundamental shots:

FOREHAND

Step out with the outside or right leg, and move over to the ball. Step into your left leg before hitting it. After making contact, step forward with the right or back leg so it's even with the front. If you're extremely rushed, get to the ball; then push off with your right leg, hit the ball, and step into the front leg. Hit the ball *after* the push off not when the weight is back on the rear leg. This is better than trying to step into that front or left leg in too much of a hurry. That would put your front leg across the back one in a closed position and put you almost totally out of position to recover for the next shot.

BACKHAND

Step out with the left leg when you start to move. Whether you hit the ball running or standing, step into your front or right leg. After you've gone through the ball, step forward with the back or left leg so it comes up even with the front one, then recover. Do not attempt recovery until your feet are even.

VOLLEY

Be sure you play this shot up with your feet always moving. For the forehand volley step forward and over toward the net with your left foot, and hit off it. For the backhand volley step over with your right foot toward the net, and hit off that one.

HALF VOLLEY

Take little quick steps and get your weight forward onto your front leg: For the forehand half volley hit off the left leg; for the backhand, off the right.

OVERHEAD

Turning to the right side, move quickly to get to a position where the ball is to the right of and in front of you. Step forward and hit this shot off your front (left) leg and follow through with your right foot coming into the court. When trapped and faced with a rapidly oncoming ball, use the scissors kick. Push off your right leg, jump into the air, hit, land on your left leg with the right one up and in front of you.

PASSING SHOT

Try to go out to the ball and catch it on the rise. For the forehand you will usually be running, so you should hit off your right leg. Push off with that leg going in the direction of the hit, and then bring it up about even with the left after you've completed the shot. On the backhand side hit off your right leg, and then step forward with the left.

APPROACH SHOT

For the forehand step forward with your right leg, hit the ball, and continue running to the net. For the backhand also step forward and hit off that right leg;

then hop forward onto that same leg. The only time to hit the approach shot off the left leg is when you're running hard for a low shot.

LOB

Step forward and hit off the left leg for a forehand offensive lob. For the backhand offensive lob step forward, and hit off the right leg. For defensive lobs fall back, and hit off the right or back leg for your forehand and off the back or left leg for the backhand.

RETURN SERVE

On the forehand side step out with your right leg, and push off to hit, catching your weight on the left leg. For the backhand return step out with your left leg and forward onto the right leg, and hit off it. Then step forward with the back leg. Let momentum carry you into the court; then recover.

SERVE

Begin with your weight forward on your front or left leg as you bounce the ball; then go to the back leg for your ready position. When you start to serve, move that weight to the front left leg again, and then push up into the air, hit, and bring the right leg forward quickly landing on it in the court.

DROP SHOT

For both forehand and backhand drop shots, run forward and get underneath the ball; then hit it off your forward leg.

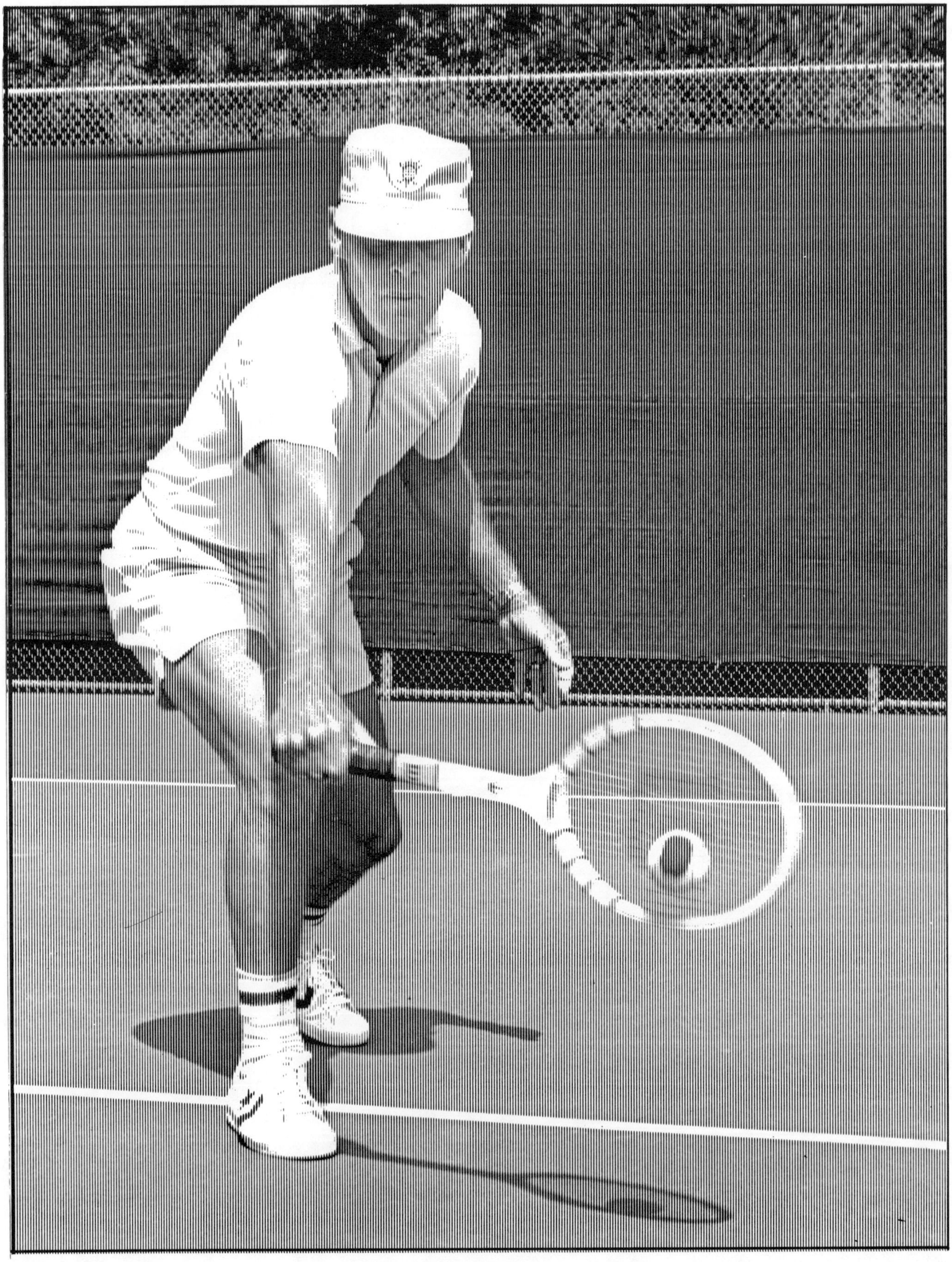

5. Equipment

One old-time player who now runs a tennis clinic says, "I'm continually asked what racket a player should use. It doesn't make any difference. They're all engineered to play a better game than you can." It usually gets a laugh, but it doesn't go very far in answering the player's question.

RACKETS

I agree that all rackets are well engineered, but I don't agree that any player can play his best with any given racket. There are too many types, materials, weights, and sizes these days not to take advantage of a racket "just for you." I've seen a change of racket weight or balance or material or even string tension change a player's game dramatically. For that reason, I'd like to spend several pages on racket selection and care and even offer a few inside tips used by pros and advanced amateurs.

Wilson, Yonex, Head, Spaulding, Dunlop, and at least a dozen other manufacturers all turn out good rackets in various models for players of different calibers. Like the fellow I quoted above, I won't pick out a brand name for you, but I will tell you what to look for before buying one. Buy a good racket. Yes, you can save money by purchasing an inexpensive one to "try," or if you're a beginner, to see if you even like the game. The trouble is that cheap or bad rackets can contribute to a bad game, resulting in discouragement with the racket and with tennis. Also, bad rackets wear out fast, and your initial economy is wasted after all. People who play a great deal of tennis generally own two rackets of similar weight, and alternate them so the action stays similar as the rackets wear. Should one break, they have the other to play with until it is repaired.

There are stiff rackets, whippy rackets,

light rackets, heavy rackets, rackets that are light or heavy in the head. There are different weights and different grip sizes. There are round heads and oval heads, and one new racket even has a head about twice the size of a regular racket and is perfectly legal to use. To top it off, there are rackets made of wood, aluminum, steel, fiberglass, graphite, and combinations of these. Out of all of that choice comes confusion. Let's try to clear up some of it.

Stiff rackets generally control the ball better.

Whippy rackets generally give more power and a better serve.

Heavy rackets usually hit the best ground strokes.

Light rackets move faster for volleys and serves.

Head-heavy rackets hit the ball harder.

Head-light rackets can be moved faster for serves and volleys.

Wooden rackets give the most feel and absorb shock.

Metal rackets move fast and last a long time but transmit shock.

Fiberglass and graphite rackets move fast, are durable, but are still in developmental stages.

Metal, graphite, and fiberglass are also expensive, so you may want to carefully consider your choice of one of these. If you're just starting out, I think it's better to begin with a light racket, something that weighs between 13 and 13¼ ounces. Medium weight rackets run between 13¼ to 13¾ ounces and heavy rackets are 14 to 15 ounces or more. The heavier the racket the stronger you should be to play it, because that weight will begin to strain your arm and hand over a series of sets.

To check a racket for balance, hold it horizontally and lightly at the throat to see which way it wants to tip. Remember, head-heavies hit harder, but head-lights are easier to whip around and handle.

As if you don't have enough decisions to make, there are different shapes and sizes of handles from which to choose. Sizes run from four to five inches in circumference. Some people measure from the lifeline of their hand to the top of the ring finger to decide the correct size. Others go strictly by comfort and feel. Beginners seem to do best with a smaller grip because it gives them better control. In addition to grip size, there's also the problem of grip shape. I like the oblong grip because I can really feel the racket, especially in my forehand strokes. However, some other players like the round grip, and even others like the square ones. It's all based on individual reaction to the feel and security that you get when holding onto the racket. I'm sorry to see the tapered grip disappearing. This one starts off smaller and gets larger as it goes toward the end of the racket. It helps prevent the racket from slipping out of your hand. Not many manufacturers seem to be making this anymore.

In addition to the sort of standardized twenty-seven-inch racket you can also buy shorter ones. I recommend these to beginners, players who have trouble getting their racket around, and children. Some players develop amazing games with these shorter rackets.

Grips are covered in leather, plastic, composition, and new rubberized materials. You'll notice also that some grips are perforated, whereas others have ridges or indentations to help you while your hand is sweating. This is a common problem, but there are quite a few solutions. Most people use a wrist sweatband to help. I know one player who has the leather grip on his Wilson mounted inside out so the rough leather is outside. He claims this absorbs perspiration and also gives him a more secure hold. Some players use sawdust or commercial no-slip preparations. Increasingly popular is the tennis glove, which absorbs and also provides grip security. The best gloves seem to be those without fingers, like a golf glove, so you don't lose feel. People whose hands get sore or blister easily should try these gloves.

The grip is so important that some top players spend hours working on it. Pancho Gonzalez is never without hammer, nails, and tape which he uses to constantly readjust the feel and fit of his grip. Another top player, who uses a wooden racket, is often seen whittling away at the handle of a new one to adjust it perfectly to his hand.

String, material, and tension strength should be chosen based on your game. Most intermediate and advanced players like gut because it seems to provide a better feel of the ball and holds the ball on the racket longer and more securely. Gut has disadvantages. It's more expensive initially, and it tends to loosen and sag when there is a great deal of moisture in the air. The synthetics are ideal for beginners and most intermediates. They're strong, durable, inexpensive, and they play almost as well as gut. Their major disadvantage is a tendency to break without warning. Gut shows wear so you can anticipate upcoming trouble. Both nylon and gut can be strung to different poundages. The more tightly strung your racket is the more rebound the ball will get from the strings. Most top players using gut have their racket strung tightly (sixty to sixty-five pounds) to get maximum power on each shot, but remember, *they* can control the ball. A new player with synthetic strings will probably find forty-five to fifty-five pounds more satisfactory all around. One warning: Don't blame your game on the racket. Tennis clubs are full of intermediate players who spend hundreds of dollars every year buying "new improved" rackets in an attempt to get a "new improved" game. I know one airline pilot who has a standing order at his club pro shop for every new racket that comes in; yet his game never seems to improve. If he spent the same amount of money on advanced lessons from a good tennis pro, he'd probably be better off. This doesn't mean you can't change rackets. When you get good with wood, for example, try out the new metal or graphite or fiberglass models. Just don't depend upon that single change to turn you from a hit and miss player into an Arthur Ashe. Make sure you keep all rackets in a cover to protect the strings and wooden rackets in a press to prevent warpage.

TENNIS BALLS

The type of tennis balls you use *can* make a difference in your game. Obviously, old balls lose some of their fuzz and some of their bounce—vital factors in the way the ball plays off your racket and off the ground. However, don't throw away old balls until you can drop them, and they just lie there instead of rebounding. Instead, keep a sack of them around for practicing. There's nothing more wearisome than having to walk around to the other side of the court and retrieve balls after hitting only two or three practice shots. Too, there are new rejuvenating-type cans that repressurize the balls, keeping them fresh and bouncy for a long time. There are also fuzzing machines that restore the ball's nap. Tennis balls come in two types: Championship and Heavy Duty. The Championship type is faster and better for slow courts. Heavy Duties are ideal for fast courts and for playing at higher altitudes. Balls are softer now than they used to be, and I believe this makes for a better tennis game. With today's balls, you can use strategy a bit more and get involved in long rallies that help develop your game.

SHOES

Playing tennis with jogging shoes or ordinary sneakers is like playing the game with a squash racket instead of a tennis racket. It can be done, but why penalize yourself by not using the equipment best for the game? There are many excellent brands of tennis shoes on the market, and they've all been designed for the sudden starts, stops, twists, and foot actions this game demands. Like the racket, the choice of shoes is up to you. Make sure they fit properly. Instead of merely walking around the shoe department after you try them on, jump, run, skip, hop, and come to sudden stops. You may look odd to other shoppers, but that's better than developing blisters or getting jammed toes because you picked a size that felt good for a few steps but all wrong for active competition. While you're buying one pair, buy two if you can afford it, especially if you're going to play a great deal. If your shoes don't get a chance to rest and dry out, they'll not only wear faster but can give you athlete's foot or other foot ailments. The shoes you select should be light but should also have good thick soles and a deep tread to help you stop quickly. Reinforced toes are important because of those sudden stops. They keep the front of the shoe from wearing out prematurely. Also make sure the shoe is sturdily constructed, gives you good support, and has a strong arch that won't break down under constant pounding. Players who have narrow feet seem to like the models that lace to the toes but if you have an average foot, the ones that lace only partway down may be fine. So far as material is concerned, pick canvas for hot weather playing. It "breathes" and allows your feet to stay somewhat dry, which makes for comfort and helps you avoid infections and fungi. Leather and synthetic materials last longer but shouldn't be used in hot weather because they do keep the heat and moisture trapped inside the shoe. For cooler weather, all materials are good.

CLOTHING

There was a time when tennis clothing was manufactured only by sporting goods people but with the increasing popularity of the game many all-purpose clothing manufacturers are turning out what they call *tennis togs*. This is both good and bad. The good is that these new lines are highly styled, smart looking, and, as you've noticed, very colorful. There is hardly a shade, including day-glo orange, that you can't get these days. Some observers feel that these new fashions are partially responsible for the increasing popularity of the game, especially among women. Tennis outfits are highly attractive, and the new designs, colors, and imaginative trim only adds to that overall effect. Maybe I'm a traditionalist, but I still like white because it reflects heat. The dark colors may be dramatic, but they absorb heat and can drain your energy on a warm, sunny day. Although some of the new clothing is very attractive, it may not be specifically designed for the game. In their attempts to ride the tennis trend, a few manufacturers have merely redone a standard line of clothing and called it tennis wear. Unfortunately, these lines aren't designed for the stretching and reaching that tennis demands. Conversely, some lines have special elastic or expandable inserts, slits, pleats, and other devices to give your body total freedom of movement. Check before you buy to make sure the clothing is not only attractive but that it won't bind, cramp, or chafe you. Cotton keeps you coolest. Man-made fabrics tend to hold in the heat and do not allow perspiration to evaporate.

In addition to dresses or shorts and tops for women and shorts and shirts for men, tennis wardrobes should also include a good warm-up suit. These outfits are ideal for playing in cooler weather or for warming up at any time. They also help to prevent chills after a hot, sweaty game. For cool weather, you should also have a couple of sweaters, wearing both of them while you warm up and then removing them one at a time as you work up a sweat.

For comfort and also if you have a tendency to blister, try wearing two pairs of socks instead of one. Ideally, the inside pair should be light cotton and the outer pair wool. This is the best combination for foot comfort and sweat absorption. If you like the new partially synthetic socks, wear them on the outside, but remember, man-made materials generally don't absorb perspiration. Take a tip from Johnny Wooden, the famous UCLA basketball coach. He used to spend an entire afternoon teaching his players how to put on their socks and shoes so they wouldn't give blisters. Make sure you adjust them smoothly and tightly before donning your shoes, and then make sure you lace those shoes so they are secure but not binding.

OTHER EQUIPMENT

You'll notice that many players have a special bag in which they carry not only rackets and balls but additional gear for their game. These bags generally contain sweat bands for the wrist and sometimes for the forehead, a hat or visor, a towel, a handkerchief to tie around the neck on especially hot days, a change of socks, shoes, or clothing, Band-aids, tape, soap, deodorants, Gauzetex or powder to apply on slippery grips, extra balls, elbow or knee braces, chewing gum, candy, sweaters or jackets, ball pressure cans, and even a jug filled with water, Gatorade, or another type of thirst-quenching liquid. These bags come in very handy and don't have to be expensive. Although fancy leather tennis totes with special pockets for the rackets, balls, etc. can be costly, I've found an ordinary, unlined, zippered nylon bag just as convenient, a great deal lighter, and easier to pack and store.

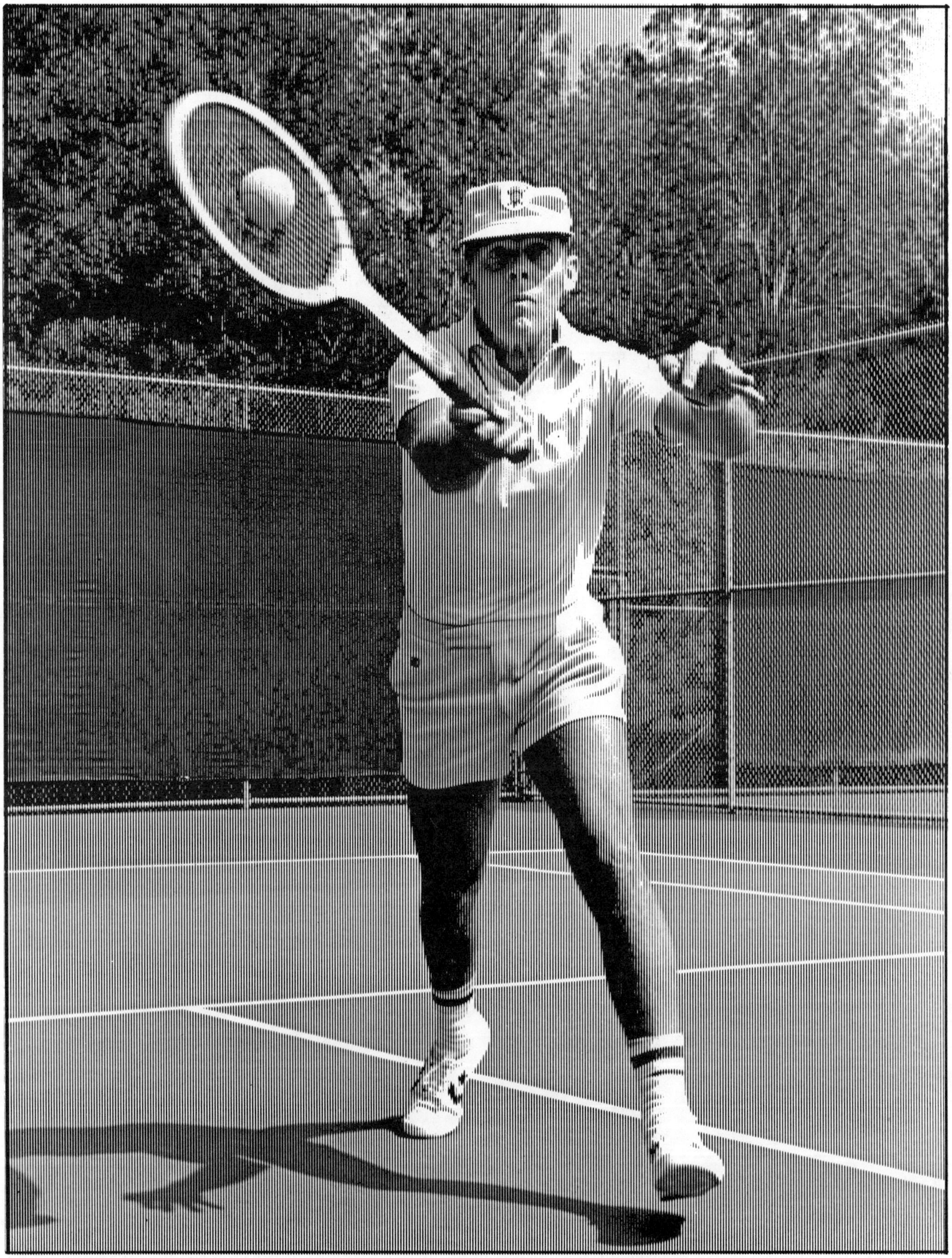

6. Secrets of Practice

There is no more important way to improve your game than by practicing the techniques we've been discussing. Through the years, I've noticed that the single major difference between two players or two teams of equal ability is how, when, and what is practiced. A player who is just out hitting but is repeating his errors may be "practicing" but certainly isn't going to improve his game. Practice should not only be used to stay in shape and to retain timing but also to concentrate upon and correct the mistakes a player is making. Players who won't practice can't possibly get better and usually get worse. It's that simple. Following are the highlights of the program we have been using to help some of the nation's finest young players develop and perfect their games. Use as much of it as you possibly can.

First, work on your wind, stamina, and endurance. Do wind sprints every other day. Sprint from the back fence up to the net, and then go backwards to the fence. Sprint from one end of the courts to the other end. Sprint sideways across the court and then back to the original position. Practice changing direction during these sprints. Start out slowly and build speed. On alternate days go in for long distance running. You can do laps on a school track or run cross-country. Run far enough to get winded; then push a little farther to expand your capacity, but don't overdo it. After a short while, you'll find the combination of wind sprints and long distance running has built up your cardiovascular system and your endurance so you'll finish a match barely breathing hard.

Drilling is extremely important to your game because it builds confidence in your strokes without putting you under the pressure of a game. If you hit a correct forehand enough times in a drill you'll hit it correctly during a game. Some days, spend three to five minutes on each stroke we've covered in this book. Other days, break your drill period down into the percentage of time you use each stroke in a game. Forehand and backhand ground strokes should have more drill than, let's say, the half volley—unless you're working to perfect that shot.

For basic drills, get a partner and practice forehand to forehand, backhand to backhand, forehand to backhand, and backhand to forehand ground strokes. Practice going down the line with your backhand to your partner's forehand and then your forehand to his backhand. Following this, drill with one person at the net and the other back. Hit forehand to forehand here; then go down the line. Switch to backhand to backhand to forehand from the net position. Make sure each person is up at the net half the time and back the other half. When that's finished, work on overhead drills, lob drills, serves, returns, even angle and drop shots. Try to practice a little of every shot each time you practice.

A good drill doesn't have to be a long drill. Many players get in a complete practice session in fifteen minutes and others like to drill for up to two hours. Don't baby yourself, but don't push too much either, especially when you get tired. Just remember that you need endurance for matches and practice is one of the best ways to build it. One system that seems to work well consists of drilling for a while, then laying off for a short rest, then working on particular shots or weaknesses. A short rest can revitalize you for another drill session, so take it when you're feeling exhausted.

Sometimes you should work on a weakness without having to worry about getting the ball back to a partner. There are several excellent ways to practice in this way. If you can locate a ball machine, get on it and practice your ground strokes, backhand volleys, or whatever shot is giving you trouble.

Backboards are easy to find these days and are excellent for practicing. You can go down the line with your forehand, hit reflex volleys, and even practice overheads (by hitting into the ground and not to the board). You can even use the backboard to work on your serve and usually it returns balls better than a live partner.

Whether it's one set or three, also practice by playing. A perfect setup is to drill in the morning and then play—for practice—in the afternoon. Play games and sets sometimes, and other times vary that by playing only tie breakers or points without games or even serving ten points and then having your playing partner serve ten points. This is especially good if you have a tournament coming up and don't want to lose confidence by playing sets you might lose. Not playing games also relaxes you enough the try variations you wouldn't attempt during a match.

Set a goal for each practice session. If you're working mostly on your serve, set a percentage—like seventy-five percent of first serves—that you want to get in. Or if you're concentrating on the approach shot, set a number you'd like to hit correctly, and try to hit that goal.

For team or serious tournament players, these morning-afternoon double sessions seem to accelerate improvement. These double sessions shouldn't be done every day because you can burn yourself out physically or even lose mental incentive to play the game. Two or three double sessions a week seem to be the best program for most players. If work or school or other demands prohibit double sessions most of the time, don't miss the single session.

BASSETTIP: *When you finish prac-*

ticing or playing, take an additional five minutes to work on a weakness. For some reason, practice after playing seems to correct mistakes best.

PRACTICING FOR TOURNAMENTS

Whether you're playing club tennis, charity tennis, interschool tennis, or neighborhood tennis, some day you're going to be in a tournament or an important match you want to win. Practicing correctly can help. Here's how a great many professional and amateur tournament players get ready for a match that's particularly important to them.

Let's talk about the week before the big game or the tournament. If your showdown is on Saturday, go into double sessions and practice hard on Monday, Tuesday, and Wednesday and then taper off a bit to let your body get refreshed and relaxed. The last two days before the tournament, practice only an hour or so. Don't wear yourself out before Saturday comes by practicing hard up to the last minute.

On the day of the game, get up, have a good breakfast, then get out and rally for fifteen minutes or a half hour, hitting every shot for a given period. If the courts are busy and you can't get on them to practice, find a backboard and use it to get warmed up and ready.

After that, get off, sit down, and think about the match ahead. Think about the way the court looks, about the spectators, about your opponent. Try to imagine the sounds, the colors, the temperature, and the way you feel while you're playing tennis. Then, try to visualize the entire match. Play it point by point in your head. Imagine what you'll do when your opponent sets up a lob or a drop shot. Think about how you're going to serve to him in different situations. Play points in your imagination and, most importantly, play to win! This mental rehearsal can go a long way toward conditioning your mind to help you win.

If your game or match isn't scheduled early, beware of sitting in the sun and watching too many other matches. Both the sun and the sitting can drain your energy. Also avoid too much visiting and tennis talk with other players. This can only make your mind wander or get confused after you've invested the time concentrating on your particular match.

Some tournament players ignore the rest of the matches either entirely or at least, until they've played theirs. They go to their room or into the clubhouse and listen to music, play cards, watch television, write letters, and, in short, do anything that isn't concerned with tennis and the match coming up.

After your match, don't stand around whether you're being consoled or congratulated. Instead, cover up, visit a little bit, and then get out of there. If you stand around chatting too long, you'll get stiff, sore, and can even catch a cold as you cool off. Obviously, none of this is good for the next day's play.

Whether you won or lost there's always tomorrow. And tomorrow means another opponent, another game, perhaps another tournament. And it means practice, practice, practice. The more it means to you, the better player you'll become in the days ahead.

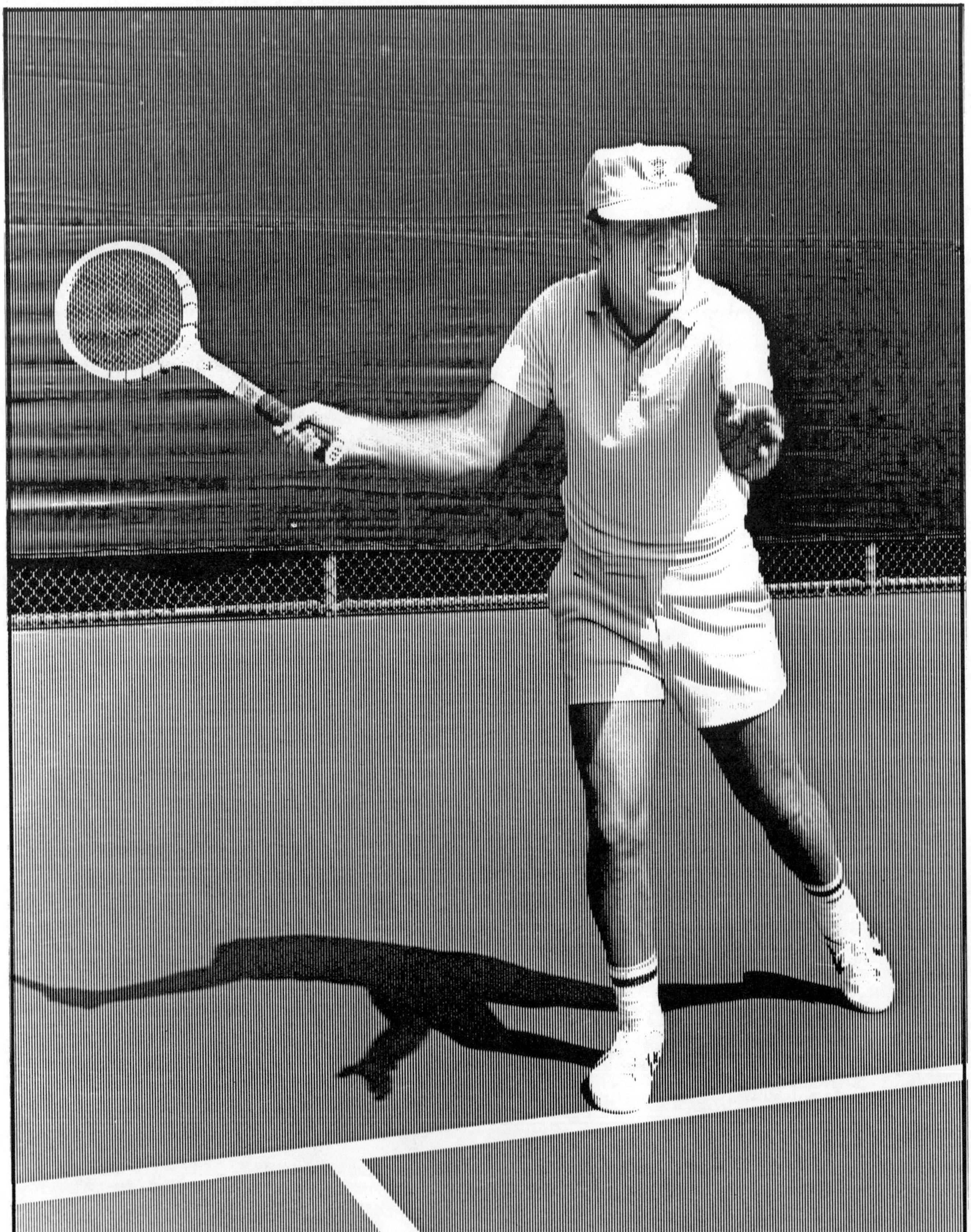

7. Questions and Answers about Winning Strategy

Some of these questions come from intercollegiate team tennis players, some from weekend players. All were selected to give a comprehensive look at the most common problems and the solutions for beginning, intermediate, and advanced players.

I used to think it was smart to beat the other guy at his own game, but I always lose. Why?

Because he's been playing it longer than you have. Don't try to beat a good server with your serve or a great ground stroker with your ground strokes. Stay with your strengths, and play your own game to start winning again.

If I'm losing a match, is there some way I can turn it around and win?

It depends upon how you're losing and why, but here are a couple of tactics you might try. First, change your game. If you're hitting hard, try hitting easier; or if you're rushing the net, start staying back to keep the ball in play. Second, slow down the pace of the game. Walk a little slower getting back into position, and take your time changing courts and getting ready to serve. Changing the pace of your shots might also work to confuse your opponent. Switch from hard to soft hits every now and then, mix them up, and keep your opponent guessing. Also, work on changing elevation of the different shots.

What is an up and back game, and is it good?

It's excellent used against beginners and intermediates. Simply put, an up and back game runs your opponent continually up to the net and then back to the back court as you mix drop shots and lobs. Most players do run well sideways but run poorly up and back. It also tires them very fast. The up and back is especially effective against good ground strokers because it forces them out of a secure comfortable stroke position and up to the net where they're apt to make a mistake.

Why should I try for depth? It seems like short shots or drop shots would be generally most effective.

Deep balls keep your opponent back in the court where he can't hurt you too badly. Only when you let him come up to the net by dropping in a short one can he get away an effective point winner. Also, hitting deep gives you time and opportunity to take the net when it's advantageous.

What is meant by a percentage game?

Simply put, it means playing the percentages by getting your first serve in, not missing strokes, and keeping the ball in play and in the court. It also means staying away from spectacular shots that have a good chance of missing or going out. Keeping the ball in play and making your opponent hit one more shot, gives you the percentage that he'll make a mistake.

How do I play a net rusher?

There are three ways to keep him from gaining control of that important spot. First, keep him in the back court by hitting deep returns from one side to the other. While he's running to retrieve those, he can't get set to come in. Second, beat him to the net every time you can. Third, if he does come in to the net, lob a lot to drive him back.

I'm an all-around better player than the guy I play against, but his steadiness beats me. Is there some way I can break up that steadiness?

It takes patience to beat a steady player. Perhaps you're feeding his steadiness by giving him exactly the ball he wants. Try changing pace, speed, and elevation on the balls you return. Slice some of them and top spin others. Use the drop shot to move him out of his comfortable position and, when you can, take the net yourself so you can pick off one of those good steady returns for a point for you.

I play one girl who lobs to me even when I'm not at the net. Why?

The lob is a much overlooked and very important offensive as well as defensive stroke. Most people use it only when they're in trouble, and that's wrong. The lob is an ideal ball for wearing your opponent down because it calls for an overhead return, and the overhead return is tiring. Also, there's nothing more demoralizing than smashing in a sure putaway return and having your opponent run it down and lob it back, especially if this happens again and again.

Is there any answer to a superb serve?

Get it back. Don't try for a putaway or a brilliant shot, but just keep the ball in play. Nothing demoralizes a good server more than having that ball returned. The psychological tendency of the server is not to credit you with the return but to start believing his serve isn't working too well today. Also, in many cases, the person who depends heavily on his serve is not ready for a return and will often miss it. This is generally true of *all defense*. The more intended putaways you can run down and get back the more upset your opponent is going to get until finally he blows a point.

Given my druthers, should I hit a down-the-line or a crosscourt return?

It depends upon the situation, but favor the crosscourt from either your forehand or backhand. It's the safer shot because the net is lower at the middle and you have more court into which to hit.

What are the best ways to play with wind or sun or both bothering me?

It's very difficult to serve properly on a windy day. Try tossing the ball a little lower so the wind can't catch it as much. If the wind is behind you, hit your serve with more top spin so it will drop into the court. Against the wind, hit it flatter because the wind will hold it in. As for bright sun, try to get your first serve in because you could be blinded for the second. When your opponent is facing the sun, lob him a great deal, and make him play the ball in the air.

How can I psych out a new opponent immediately?

By winning the first point of the first game regardless of who's serving. Play that point more intently than any other because it sets the tone for the entire match. Should things not go well, however, and you lose it, don't get discouraged. Hang tough, and don't let that point loss demoralize you. Also try to win the first game of every set to put your opponent on the defensive for the rest of the set.

Do yoga and tennis conditioning exercises go together?

Like strawberries and cream at Wimbledon. The best tennis exercises are stretching exercises which give you balance, grace, supple muscles, and strength. This is also what yoga does. The only problem I've ever found with it is that it feels so good, it can cut into practice or playing time if you do it too much.

After discovering an opponent's weakness isn't it smart to concentrate on it?

Not necessarily. The more you play that weakness, the stronger it could become. If you continue hitting to a weak backhand it might become stronger as the match goes on. The best way to handle this is to hit wide to the strength which opens up the weak-side court. Then hit to that side, and come up to the net. Don't be intimidated by an opponent's strong shot. Play his confidence in it to get him out of position.

When I'm behind a game or a set I get discouraged. Is there any way to counteract this?

You're giving the other guy the psychological advantage. Instead of losing confidence when you miss a return or a serve, look ahead to the next one. Keep talking positively to yourself. Congratulate yourself out loud after making a good point. Stay in the game and maintain a winning attitude. Also remember the trick of changing game pace. If your opponent is in a hurry and trying to rush you, slow him down by leisurely changing courts, adjusting your serve stance, retrieving balls. For the slow-moving opponent, however, hurry things up a bit. Changing the pace of the game can often change the momentum of victory.

My doubles partner breaks her neck going after every ball whether she can possibly get it or not. Is this right?

It's both good and bad. The good is that she probably saves some points by getting to seemingly impossible returns. The bad is that she's probably wearing herself out needlessly chasing balls that are on their way out. The only answer here is split-second experience and judgment. Is it possible she's going after too many difficult balls because you aren't going after enough? Perhaps you both should set up some rules on what you'll chase and what you'll let go.

Opponents don't beat me, but I beat myself with mistakes. Is there any solution?

Concentrate on your game and stop making mistakes. Here are a few tips on winning points you might be losing by playing incorrectly. Most mistakes are made when you're out of position. If you know you're going to be out of control for the next shot, then either get back a great return or get under the ball and send up a lob to give yourself time to recover. When your opponent is back and sends you a ball that comes in low, either drop shot or lob it deep so you have time to get back into position. When you're deep and he's up, lob over him. If you're missing easy shots, remember to play the ball in front of you and stay through it a little longer. If it's good opponent strategy that's upsetting your game, then revert to steadiness, and don't try for spectacular putaways. Let the opponent make the mistakes.

I like both weight lifting and tennis. Will the weights make me too bulky or muscle bound for the other sport?

Yes and no. If you're interested in building short, knotty muscles, then these can negatively affect your grace, ease of movement, and speed. However, some weight lifting is definitely recommended for tennis players. I don't encourage weights during a playing season, but I do suggest that players use them during the off season. The program we recommend concentrates upon light weights which can be moved very rapidly. Each workout consists of four or five exercises done in repeated two or three or four series. Start with barbell curls and repeat them eight to twelve times for two or three sets. Bent arm pullovers are excellent. In this exercise, lie on your back with the weight in back of your head and then lift it over until it's even with the head, arms straight. Finally, lower it to the original position. Sets and repetitions should be the same as curls. Use the prone press: lie flat and push a barbell straight up from the chest until the arms are straight, then return it to the original position. We also include squats with weight on the neck and shoulders. Don't bend your knees totally on this one because you can damage them. Finally, you should include a variety of stomach exercises including trunk curls and sit ups. Some players hold a weight on their chests or behind their necks while doing sit ups to increase the muscle workout, but be careful not to strain yourself if you do this. Remember, don't lift weights when playing a great deal, but do when you're laying off.

Can you give me a couple of strategic hints on each shot as a sort of review and something I can carry in my head during matches?

Forehand. Hit it with a top spin or flat drive but seldom, if ever, slice it. Crosscourt is a safer shot than down the line. Change pace.

Backhand. You can hit it top spin, flat, or slice. The slice usually is the safe shot. Crosscourt is easier to get in than the down the line, but mix them up.

Serve. Change pace on what you serve. Mix up flat serves, slices, and top spins. Always place the second serve to your opponent's backhand. Also move around occasionally on the baseline and serve from different location to confuse your opponent.

Return of serve. Play the server's tendencies. If he serves deep, move back; if wide, move out. Move around a lot to put pressure on the server. Slice some returns, and come over others. If the server stays back, return it deep with a regular ground stroke. If he comes in and volleys well, try a passing shot or a lob.

Volley. Hit it with back spin; the lower it comes to you the more back spin. If you're in trouble, hit it deep; but if you're in good position, take your choice of hard crosscourt, hard down-the-line, or easy angle shot. Don't try putaway volleys when you're off balance or out of position.

Half Volley. Hit it with a little top spin, and don't try to put it away. This shot is a response to a difficult situation, so just get it back and wait for another putaway opportunity.

Offensive Lob. Disguise it as a ground stroke before hitting. Hit it with top spin on the forehand side, but slice it when hitting backhand lobs most of the time. Hit to their backhand side.

Defensive Lob. Get under the ball, and get it high in the air to give yourself time to get back into court. Place it deep so it must bounce. Don't try and hit the sidelines.

Overhead. Hit it flat, deep, and down the middle if you're in trouble; otherwise, put it away. If you're rushed, use the scissors kick to get up and get to it. When the return is coming straight down, wait until it bounces. Practice both in-the-air and bounce returns.

Approach. Hit a flat or top-spin forehand down the line to the opponent's backhand or crosscourt to a left-handed player. Place it deep and come into the net prepared to volley for the putaway. Remember, the approach shot is not basically a winner but sets up the next shot. Slice the backhand approach shot, and mix down the lines and crosscourts about half and half.

Passing. Most of the time, hit these with top spin and down the line so they get quickly by your opponent. Mix in some crosscourts and angle crosscourts.

Two Handed. Wait until the last second to hit these shots. Use top spin and take your choice of crosscourts, down the lines, or angles; they're all easy with the two-handed. On the backhand, develop your slice approach shot to get into the net quicker.

Drop Shot. Play this one at or inside the service line. Fake an approach shot, then drop shot, especially if your opponent is behind his baseline. Also use this against poor volleyers or slow players when you want to bring them up to the net. Hit it low and slice both forehand and backhand drop shots. Angle or crosscourt this shot for the fast opponent and down the line for slower ones. The backhand drop can be faked better than the forehand one. Use it extensively against beginners, intermediates, and good baseline strokers. Don't use it as much against good net rushers, and good volleyers because it brings them up to their strong positions.

HOW TO WIN EVEN IF YOU LOSE

Because we live in a highly competitive society, winning has become overemphasized, and the overwhelming desire to win can actually cause you to lose. A *must win* attitude preys on your mind constantly, sets up tensions and stresses, and even affects your timing, rhythm, and body movements. Winning is not everything, and losing is not the end of everything. Sometimes when you've lost you've played better than when you've won and have definitely accomplished something for your game and yourself. Winning can be deceptive because it can give you too much confidence. The only way to continually win for yourself is to play the best possible game you can and don't worry abut the outcome. It's essential that you think like a winner but, more importantly, like a constantly growing and improving player. Set short-range goals and long-range goals. When you lose a match, think to yourself, "Okay, I lost this time, but I did win four or five games from my opponent. Next time I'm going to get six or seven or eight or nine or whatever it takes." And you will, if you think that way. For long-range goals, plan to win one more round of a tournament than you've ever done before, just one more, not the entire tournament. Eventually, you'll get that too. If you keep practicing, keep working, and keep the right emotional and mental attitudes you can become a far better player than you ever hoped to become.

It's basically very simple: As we said earlier, if you can count to four you can learn the winning strokes.

Then, if you can then count on *yourself* you can turn those strokes into a winning game.

Good luck and good hitting.

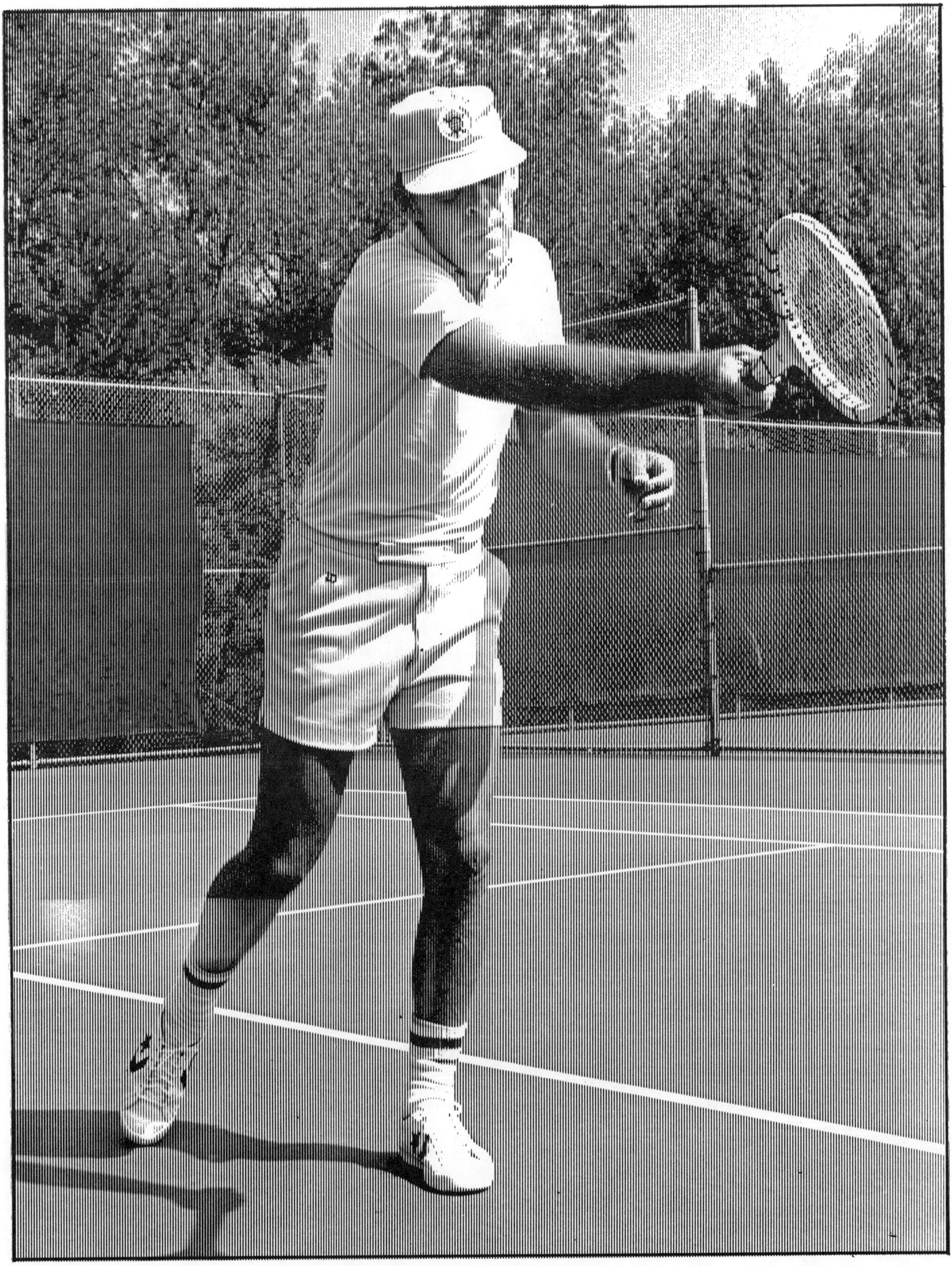

Glossary

Ace a serve that is hit so well that an opponent fails to touch it with his racket.

Ad short for advantage; it is the first point scored after deuce. If the serving side scores, it is "ad in"; if the receiving side scores, it is "ad out."

All an even score; 30-all, 3-all, etc.

Alley that area outside the singles court which enlarges the width of the court for doubles. Each alley is 4½ feet wide.

American twist a serve in which the ball bounces high and in the opposite direction from which it was originally traveling.

Angle shot a ball hit to an extreme angle across the court.

Approach shot a ground stroke behind which a player comes to the net.

Australian doubles doubles in which the point begins when the server and his partner are on the same half of the court.

Back court the area where you are playing a match from around the baseline.

Backhand the stroke used to return balls hit to the left of a right-handed player.

Backhand court the left side of the court for a right-handed player.

Backspin spin from top to bottom, applied by hitting down and through the ball; also called underspin. See also *Chop, Slice.*

Backswing the initial part of any swing; the act of bringing the racket back to prepare for the forward swing.

Ball boy a person who retrieves balls for tennis players during competition.

Baseline the end boundary line of a tennis court, located 39 feet from the net and paralleling the net.

Break service to win a game in which the opponent serves.

Bye occurs when a player is not required to play a particular round.

Cannonball a hard, flat serve.

Center mark the short line that bisects the center of the baseline.

Center service line the line which is perpendicular to the net and divides the two service courts.

Center strap a strap in the center of the net, anchored to the ground to hold the net secure.

Chip a modified slice, which requires a short swing; usually not hit hard; has underspin.

Choke to grip the racket up higher on the handle than usual.

Chop a lock spin shot that has more than the normal backspin; therefore, the racket moves down through the ball at a greater angle.

Closed face the angle of the hitting face of the racket when it is turned down toward the court.

Consolation a tournament in which losers continue to play in a loser's tournament.

Crosscourt shot a shot in which the ball travels diagonally across the net, from one corner to the other.

Deep shot or depth a shot that bounces near the baseline, also near the service line on a serve.

Default failure to complete a scheduled match in a tournament; such a player forfeits his match.

Deuce a score of 40-40 (the score is tied and each side has at least three points).

Deuce court right court, so called because a deuce score is served there.

Dink a ball hit so that if floats with extreme softness, usually very high.

Double elimination a tournament in which you must lose twice before you are eliminated.

Double fault the failure of both service attempts to be good; results in the loss of the point.

Doubles a match with four players, two on each side.

Draw the means of establishing who plays whom in a tournament.

Drive a ground stroke hit with power.

Drop shot a softly hit shot that barely travels over the net.

Drop volley a drop shot that is hit from a volley position.

Earned point a point won by skillful playing rather than a player's mistake.

Elimination after being defeated in a tournament, one can no longer participate.

Error a point which ends by an obvious mistake rather than by skillful playing.

Face the hitting surface of the racket.

Fast court a smooth-surfaced court that allows the ball to bounce quickly and low.

Fault an improper hit, generally thought of as a serve error.

Fifteen the first point won by a player.

Flat shot a shot that travels in a straight line with little arc and little spin.

Floater a ball that moves slowly across the net in a high trajectory.

Footfault a fault caused by the server stepping on or over the baseline before hitting the ball in service.

Force a ball hit with exceptional power; a play in which, because of the speed and placement of the shot, the opponent is pulled out of position.

Fore court the area between the net and the service line.

Forehand court the right side of the court for a right-handed player.

Forty a player's score when he has won three points.

Frame the part of the racket that holds the strings.

Game that part of a set that is completed when one player or side wins four points, or wins two consecutive points after deuce.

Grip the method of holding the racket handle; the term given the leather covering on the handle.

Ground strokes strokes made after the ball has bounced, either forehand or backhand.

Gut racket strings made from animal intestines.

Half volley hitting the ball immediately after it bounces off the court.

Handle the part of the racket that is gripped in the hand.

Head the part of the racket used to hit the ball; includes the frame and the strings.

Hold serve to serve and to win that game.

Kill to smash the ball hard when hitting a winner.

Let a point played over because of interference; a serve which hit the top of the net but is otherwise good.

Linesman a person responsible for calling balls that land outside the court in competition.

Lob a ball hit high enough in the air to make the net player reach up in order to hit the ball; usually hit high enough to try and get over net man's head.

Love zero; no score.

Love game a game won without the loss of a point.

Love set a set won without the loss of a game.

Match singles or doubles play that usually consists of two out of three sets; sometimes three out of five sets.

Match point the point which, if won, wins the match for a player.

Midcourt the area in the center of the playing court, midway between the net and the baseline.

Mix up to vary the type of shots selected.

Net game to play the net; also called net play.

Net man the partner in doubles who plays at the net.

No man's land midcourt, where many balls bounce at the player's feet.

Open face the hitting face of the racket when it is turned up away from the court surface.

Opening a mistake which allows an opponent a good chance to score a point.

Out a ball landing outside the playing area.

Overhead smash see *Smash*.

Over spin see *Top spin*.

Pace speed; usually referring to the speed of a ball which makes it move fast.

Passing shot a ground stroke hit, in an attempt to hit out of the reach of a net player.

Percentage tennis cutting down on unnecessary errors.

Place to hit the ball to an intended area.

Placement a shot hit so well that an opponent cannot reach it.

Poach occurs when the net player in doubles moves over into his partner's side of the court to make a volley.

Point that part of a game started by a serve and ended when a player or side wins or misses a shot.

Press a wooden or metal frame that holds a tennis racket firmly enough to prevent warping.

Rally occurs when the ball is hit back and forth over the net a number of times; can occur in practice or matches.

Retrieve returning a very difficult shot.

Round robin a tournament in which every player plays every other player.

Rush to move to the net after hitting a shot.

Seed to arrange a tournament so that the top players don't play against each other until the final rounds.

Serve (service) the shot that starts a point.

Service line the line that is parallel to and twenty-one feet from the net.

Set the part of a match that is completed when one player or side wins at least six games and is ahead by at least two games, or when one player has won the tie breaker.

Set point the point which, if won, will win the set.

Side spin a shot that, when hit, spins to the side and bounces to the side.

Singles a match between two players.

Slice a shot hit with backspin; your racket hits the ball when traveling down through the ball. This shot has less spin and more power than the chip or chop.

Slow court a court which makes the ball bounce slower and higher.

Smash a hard shot hit at the net, usually an overhead shot.

Spin the hitting of the ball at an angle causing the ball to rotate in an unusual manner; see *Top spin, Slice, Side spin, Backspin*.

Straight sets to win a match without the loss of a set.

Tape the band which runs across the top of the net.

Tennis elbow a condition in the elbow caused by undue pressure or strain; common to tennis players and is very painful.

Thirty the second point won by a player in a game.

Throat that part of the racket between the handle and the head.

Tie break an official nine-point, twelve-point, or thirteen-point sudden death scoring system when the score is tied at games-all.

Top spin spin of the ball from top to bottom; caused by hitting up and through the ball. It makes the ball bounce fast and high.

Trajectory the angle of the ball in relation to its contact with the racket and the flight of the ball over the top of the net; how high it goes over the top of net.

Umpire that person who officiates at matches.

Undercut see *Backspin, Chip, Chop, Slice*.

Underspin see *Backspin, Chip, Chop, Slice*.

Unseeded those players who are not favored to win a tournament; they are not given any special placing in the draw.

VASSS a 31-point scoring system.

Volley to hit the ball before it bounces.

Wood shot a ball hit on the frame of the racket.

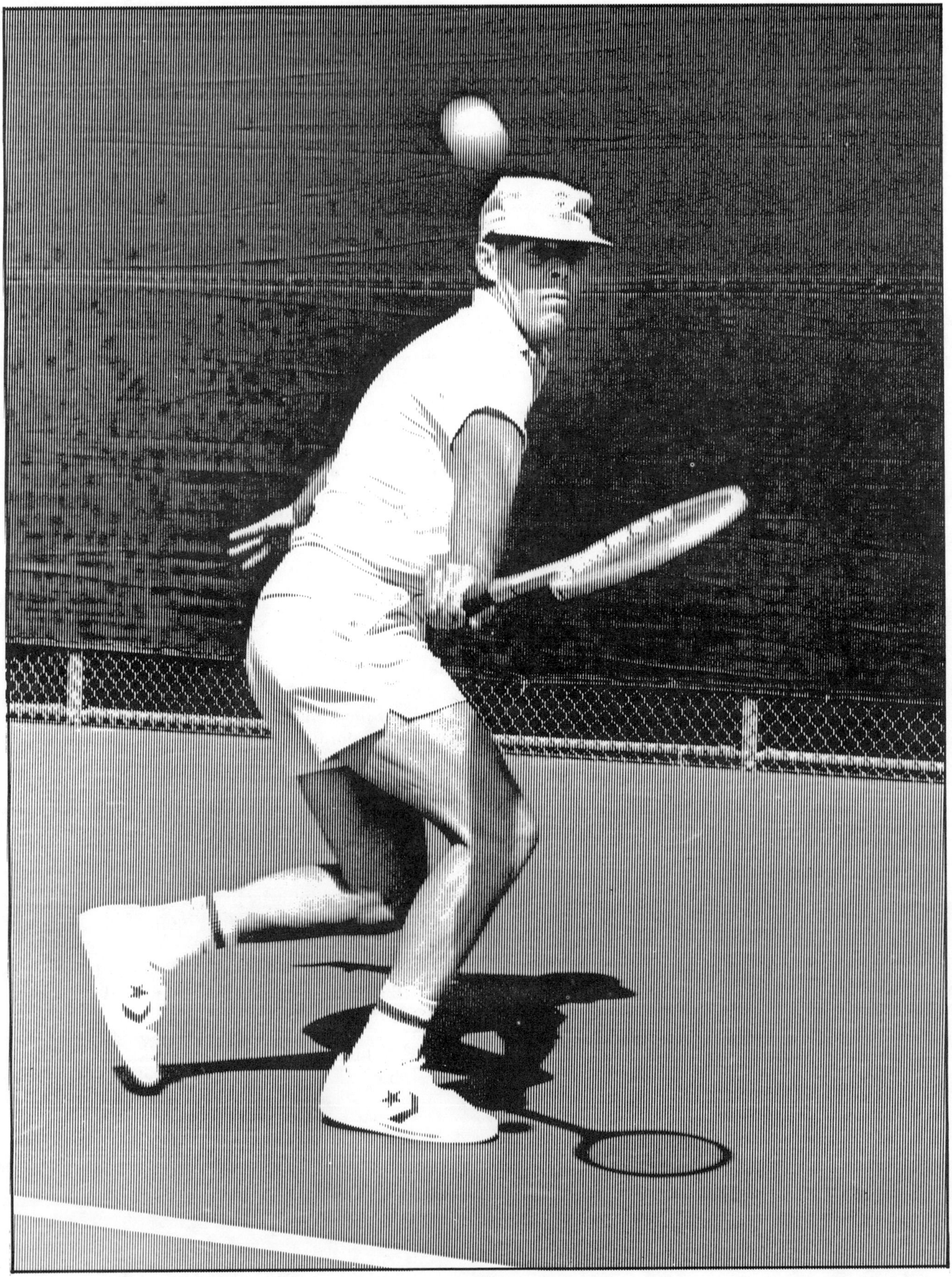

Index

A

Ace, 99
Ad in, ad out, 99
All, 99
Alley, 99
American twist, 99
Angle shot, 99
Approach shot, 29-31, 99, *illus.* 28, 29, 30
   backswing, 28-29
   follow through, 31
   hit, 29-31
   step, 29, 80-81
   strategy, 31, 76-77, 97
Ashe, Arthur, 70
Austin, Jeff, 67
Australian doubles, 99

B

Back court, 99
   rallies, 75-76
Back spin, 31, 59-60, 99
Backboards for practice, 90, 91
Backhand, 1, 8-13, 90, 96, 99
   approach shots, 28, *illus.* 28
   backcourt rallies, 75
   backswing, 9-10, *illus.* 9
   follow through, 12-13, *illus.* 13
   grip, 8-9
   half volley, 64-67, *illus.* 65, 66
   hit, 11-12, *illus.* 11
   position, 76
   return, 49, 53-54, *illus.* 51, 52, 53
   step, 10, 80, 81, *illus.* 10
   two-handed stroke, 37-39, *illus.* 38, 39
   volley, 61-64, *illus.* 61, 62, 63
Backhand court, 99
Backhand overhead, 70
Backhand slice, 13-15, 28, *illus.* 14-15
Backswing, 99
   approach shots, 28-29, *illus.* 28
   backhand, 9-10, *illus.* 9
   figure eight, 4, 9
   forehand, 3-5, *illus.* 4
   half volley, 64, *illus.* 65
   passing shots, 17, *illus.* 18
   on returns, *illus.* 51
   serve, 43, *illus.* 44
   smash, 67, *illus.* 68
   two-handed, 36, 37, *illus.* 36, 38
   volley, 58-59, 61, *illus.* 58, 61
Ball boy, 99
Ball machine, 90

Balls, 85-86
Baseline, 99
Borowiak, Jeff, 70
Break service, 99
Bye, 99

C

Cannonball, 17, 99
Center mark, 99
Center service line, 99
Center strap, 99
Chip, 99
Choke, 100
Chop, 100
Clay court tennis, 3, 17
Closed face, 100
Clothing, 86-87
College tennis, 73
Conditioning, 89, 95, 96
Connors, Jimmy, 34, 39, 49, 57, 69, 70, 77, 79
Consolation, 100
Continental grip, 2, 8-9, 42, 58, 61, 67, *illus.* 2, 8
Court, Margaret, 70
Court position, 48, 50, 73-77
Crosscourt shot, 5, 6, 11, 16, 28, 34, 74, 75, 94, 96
Crossover, 79, *illus.* 78

D

Deep shot (depth), 94, 100
Default, 100
Depth perception, 34
Deuce, 100
Deuce court, 100
Dink, 100
Double elimination, 100
Double fault, 100
Doubles, 100
Doubles, Australian, 99
Down-the-line shot, 6, 11, 16, 28, 34, 74, 75, 94, 96
Draw, 100
Drive, 100
Drop shot, 31-34, 81, 100, *illus.* 32-33
　strategy, 33-34, 74, 75, 76, 97
Drop volley, 100

E

Earned point, 100
Eastern backhand grip, 9, 61, *illus.* 8
Eastern grip, 2, 58, 67, *illus.* 2
Elimination, 100

Error, 100
Evert, Chris, 34
Exercises, 89, 95, 96

F

Face, 100
Fast court, 100
Fault, 100
Fiberglass rackets, 84
Fifteen, 100
Flat shot, 9, 100
Flat serve, 44-45
Fleming, Peter, 70
Floater, 100
Foot fault, 100
Footwork, 77-81
　approach shot, 31, 80-81
　backhand, 10, 80
　drop shot, 81
　forehand, 5, 80
　ground strokes, 78-79
　half volley, 80
　lob, 81
　passing shot, 17, 80
　serve, 81
　serve return, 50, 81
　smash, 69, 80
　volley, 60, 63, 80
Force, 100
Fore court, 100
Forehand, 1-8, 75, 90, 96
　approach shots, 27-28, *illus.* 28, 29
　backswing, 3-5, *illus.* 4
　follow through, 6-8, *illus.* 7
　grip, 1-3, 7, 42, 67, *illus.* 2-3
　half volley, 64-67, *illus.* 65, 66
　hit, 5-6, *illus.* 6
　position, 76
　returns, 48, 49, 51-53, *illus.* 51, 52, 53
　step, 5, 80, *illus.* 5
　two-handed stroke, 34-37, *illus.* 36, 37
　volley, 58-61, *illus.* 58, 59
Forehand court, 100
Forty, 100
Fox, Alan, 65
Frame, 100

G

Game, 100
Gear, 87
Glove, 85
Gonzales, Pancho, 49, 85

Graphite rackets, 84
Grip, 35, 100
    backhand, 8-9
    forehand, 1-3, *illus.* 2-3
    racket design, 84-85
    service, 42
    two-handed, 35-36, 37
    volley, 58, 61
Ground strokes, 1-39, 100
    backhand slice, 13-15, *illus.* 14-15
    on returns, 47-48
    strategy, 74
Gut, 85, 100

H

Half volley, 64-67, 76, 80, 96, 100, *illus.* 66
Handle, 100
Hard-hit crosscourt shot, 16
Head, 100
Hold serve, 100

K

Kill, 100
Kreiss, Bobby, 57

L

Laver, Rod, 41
Let, 100
Linesman, 100
Lob, 20-27, 77, 94, 100
    backswing, 21, 25, *illus.* 21, 24
    defensive, 21-25, 96-97, *illus.* 21, 22, 23
    follow through, 22-23, 26, *illus.* 23, 26
    hit, 22, 26, *illus.* 22, 25
    offensive, 25-27, 96, *illus.* 24, 25, 26
    returning, 69, 74
    on serve returns, 50
    step, 21-22, 25-26, 81, *illus.* 22, 24
    strategy, 23-24, 27
Long distance running, 89
Love, 100
Love game, 100
Love set, 100
Low, short crosscourt shot, 16
Lutz, Bob, 67

M

Martin, Billy, 39, 57, 69, 70, 77
Match, 100
Match point, 100

Material of racket, 84
Mental preparation, 91
Metal rackets, 84
Midcourt, 100
Mix up, 100

N

Net game, 101
Net man, 101
Newcombe, John, 42
No man's land, 101

O

Open face, 101
Opening, 101
Out, 101
Over spin. *See* Top spin
Overhead smash, 67-70, 76, 80, 94, 97, 101, *illus.* 68
    backhand overhead, 70

P

Pace, 101
Passing shot, 15-20, 25-27, 77, 80, 97, 101, *illus.* 18-19, 20
Percentage tennis, 94, 101
Physical fitness, 89, 95, 96
Place, 101
Placement, 101
Poach, 101
Point, 101
Positioning your strengths, 74
Practice, 89-91
    half volley, 65-67, 90
Press, 101
Psyching the opponent, 95

R

Racket, 83-85
Rallies, 75-76, 101
    back court, 75-76
    net-back court, 76
Retrieve, 101
Returns, service, 47-54, 81, 94, 96
    aiming, 49-50
    backhand, 49, 53-54, *illus.* 51, 52, 53
    forehand, 49, 51-53, *illus.* 51, 52, 53
    position, 48-49, 50, 77
Riggs, Bobby, 70
Rose, Gary, 67
Rosewall, Ken, 49
Round robin, 101
Rush, 101

S

Scissors kick, 69, 97
Seed, 101
Segura, Pancho, 34
Service (serve), 41-54, 101, *illus.* 44, 45, 46
  back swing, 43
  elbow bend, 43-44
  flat serve, 44-45
  follow through, 45-46
  grip, 42
  hit, 44
  practice techniques, 46, 90
  returns, 47-54, 77, 81, 94, 96
  slice, 45
  stance, 42, 81
  strategy, 46-47, 77, 96
  top spin, 45
Service line, 101
Set, 101
Set point, 101
Shoes, 86
Side spin, 101
Singles, 101
Size of racket, 84
Slice, 9, 27-28, 74, 96, 101
  backhand, 13-15, 62, *illus.* 14-15
  serve, 45
  serve return, 49, 54
Slide-skip, 79, *illus.* 78
Slow court, 101
Smash, overhead, 67-70, 76, 80, 94, 97, 101, *illus.* 68
  backhand overhead, 70
Smith, Stan, 42, 67
Socks, 87
Solomon, Harold, 39
Spin, 101
Sprint, 79, 89 *illus.* 79
Straight sets, 101
Strategy, 93-97
  approach shots, 31
  drop shots, 33-34
  lobs, 23-25, 27
  passing shots, 19-20
  service, 46-47
  smash, 69-70
  volley, 60-61, 63-64
Sun interference, 94-95

T

Tape, 101
Target practice, 46
Tennis balls, 85-86
Tennis elbow, 35, 101
Tennis togs, 86
Tension, racket, 85
Thirty, 101
Throat, 101
Tie break, 101
Top spin, 3, 5, 7, 9, 12, 16-17, 101
  serve, 45
Tote bags, 87
Tournament preparation, 91
Trajectory, 101
Two-handed stroke, 34-39, 97, *illus.* 36, 37, 38, 39
  backhand, 37-39, *illus.* 38, 39
  backswing, 36, 37-38
  follow through, 37, 38-39
  forehand, 34-37, *illus.* 36, 37
  grip, 35-36, 37
  hit, 36-37, 38
  step, 36, 38

U

Umpire, 101
Undercut, 101
Underspin (backspin), 99, 101
Unseeded, 101
Up and back game, 93

V

VanderMeer, Dennis, 70
VASSS, 101
Volley, 57-64, 101
  backhand, 61-64, *illus.* 61, 62, 63
  backswing, 58-59, 61
  follow through, 60, 62-63
  footwork, 60, 63, 80
  hit, 59-60, 62
  position, 76
  step, 59, 61-62
  strategy, 60-61, 63-64, 96

W

Warm-up outfit, 87
Warpage, 85
Weight lifting, 96
Weight of racket, 84
Western grip, 2-3, *illus.* 3
Wind factor, 94
Wind sprints, 89
Wooden rackets, 84
Wood shot, 101

Y

Yoga exercises, 95